Butterflies that have pron

Butterflies that have pron

Butterflies
OF **OHIO**
FIELD GUIDE

by Jaret C. Daniels

Adventure Publications, Inc.
Cambridge, MN

ACKNOWLEDGEMENTS:

I would like to thank my wife, Stephanie, for her unending patience dealing with the countless number of caterpillars, butterflies and associated plant material that happens to always find a way into our home. Thanks to my parents for encouraging my early interest in biology.

Photo credits by photographer and page number:
Cover photo: Baltimore Checkerspot by Randy Emmitt
Thomas J. Allen: 40 (larva), 42 (larva), 44 (ventral, larva), 62 (larva), 72 (larva), 80 (larva), 82 (larva), 88 (larva), 92 (larva), 94 (larva), 96 (larva), 100 (larva), 104 (larva), 108 (larva), 112 (larva), 114 (larva), 118 (larva), 120 (larva), 122 (larva), 124 (larva), 126 (larva), 128 (larva), 130 (larva), 132 (larva), 134 (larva), 136 (larva), 142 (larva), 144 (larva), 146 (larva), 150 (larva), 152 (larva), 154 (larva), 156 (larva), 158 (larva), 164 (larva), 170 (larva), 174 (larva), 176 (larva), 178 (larva), 180 (larva), 184 (larva), 190 (larva), 192 (larva), 198 (larva), 202 (larva), 210 (larva), 212 (larva), 218 (larva), 222 (larva), 224 (larva), 232 (larva), 236 (larva), 238 (larva), 240 (larva), 246 (larva), 256 (larva), 258 (larva), 260 (larva), 264 (larva), 268 (larva), 270 (larva), 272 (larva), 284 (larva), 286 (larva), 294 (larva), 296 (larva), 298 (larva), 306 (larva), 316 (larva) **ATL (Elton Woodbury Collection):** 90 (both), 96 (ventral), 102 (larva), 116 (ventral), 168 (larva), 264 (male dorsal), 266 (ventral), 282 (larva), 310 (ventral) **Susan Borkin:** 228 (all) **Rick & Nora Bowers/BowersPhoto.com:** 40 (dorsal), 42 (dorsal, ventral), 62 (male ventral), 68 (male dorsal), 70 (larva), 84 (female), 86 (female), 94 (male dorsal), 124 (dorsal), 132 (female dorsal), 138 (male dorsal), 156 (dorsal, ventral), 162 (all), 170 (ventral), 176 (dorsal), 186 (larva), 194 (dorsal), 235 (male dorsal), 240 (female), 244 (dorsal), 248 (male ventral), 298 (female, ventral) **Jay Cossey:** 64 (ventral), 74 (male), 78 (all), 190 (dorsal), 224 (dorsal), 252 (female), 306 (dorsal), 308 (dorsal) **Randy Emmitt/www.RLEPhoto.com:** 40 (ventral), 44 (dorsal), 54 (ventral), 66 (male ventral), 72 (ventral), 76 (male, ventral), 80 (ventral), 100 (ventral), 102 (male, female), 108 (ventral), 110, 112 (ventral, male, female), 120 (dorsal), 126 (female ventral, female, male dorsal), 128 (ventral, dorsal), 130 (dorsal), 136 (ventral, male), 140, 148 (both), 152 (dorsal), 154 (female), 158 (male), 164 (female dorsal), 168 (male, female), 170 (male, female), 172, 174 (ventral, dorsal), 178 (ventral, male), 186 (dorsal), 192 (dorsal, ventral), 198 (ventral), 202 (larva), 206 (dorsal), 216, 220 (ventral), 224 (ventral), 226 (both), 232 (male dorsal, female dorsal), 242 (male ventral), 246 (ventral, female), 250 (ventral), 256 (male, female), 260 (ventral, male, female), 264 (male ventral), 270 (ventral, male), 282 (summer, winter), 286 (ventral), 302 (male dorsal), 306 (ventral), 310 (male, female) **Jeff M. Fengler:** 150 (dorsal) **Jeffrey Glassberg:** 144 (male), 212 (male), 218 (female ventral, female dorsal) **Paul A. Opler:** 144 (ventral) **David K. Parshall:** 104 (male), 122 (female dorsal), 150 (ventral) **Jeff Pippen:** 146 (dorsal, ventral) **Jane Ruffin:** 104 (ventral), 122 (male ventral, male dorsal, female variant), 230 (female) **John & Gloria Tveten:** 48 (all), 50 (all), 58 (larva), 66 (dark-form female ventral), 68 (larva), 70 (ventral), 72 (male), 74 (female), 76 (larva), 88 (ventral), 92 (dorsal, ventral), 98 (green larva, red larva), 100 (larva), 106 (larvae), 116 (larva), 120 (ventral), 138 (larva), 142 (male), 164 (female "Pocahontas" ventral, ventral), 166 (female ventral, larva), 182 (all), 184 (dorsal, ventral), 198 (ventral), 206 (ventral), 220 (larva), 222 (larva), 232 (male ventral), 236 (dorsal), 240 (ventral), 254 (male), 258 (ventral), 262 (ventral), 266 (male, larva), 268 (male, male ventral), 272 (ventral, dorsal), 276 (male, female, larva), 286 (dorsal), 288 (larva), 290 (larva), 294 (ventral), 308 (ventral, larva), 310 (larva), 314 (male), 322 (male dorsal), 324 (male dorsal), 326 (male), 328 (female dorsal) **John & Gloria Tveten/KAC Productions:** 130 (ventral), 180 (ventral) **Jaret C. Daniels:** all other photos

Book and Cover Design by Jonathan Norberg
Illustrations by Julie Martinez
Range Maps and Phenograms by Anthony Hertzel
Thanks to Mr. David Parshall, president of the Ohio Lepidopterists, who generously agreed to review the manuscript and provided a wealth of beneficial suggestions.

TABLE OF CONTENTS

WATCHING BUTTERFLIES IN OHIO

People are rapidly discovering the joy of butterfly gardening and watching. Both are simple, fun and rewarding ways to explore the natural world and bring the beauty of nature closer. Few other forms of wildlife are more attractive or as easily observed as butterflies. Butterflies occur just about everywhere. They can be found from suburban gardens and urban parks to rural meadows and remote natural areas. So regardless of where you may live, there are a variety of butterflies to be seen. *Butterflies of Ohio Field Guide* is for those who wish to identify and learn more about the many different butterflies found in Ohio.

There are more than 725 species of butterflies in North America north of Mexico. While the majority of these are regular breeding residents, still others show up from time to time as rare tropical strays. In Ohio, over 135 different butterflies have been recorded. Within that mix, there are widespread representatives that occur commonly over a large portion of the continent and others that are rare or limited to only a few localized areas, including two federally endangered species. Although such numbers pale in comparison to many tropical countries, Ohio boasts a rich and diverse butterfly fauna. To aid in your exploration, this field guide covers all resident and stray species recorded within the state.

Despite its small size, with a total land area of just over 44,000 square miles, Ohio boasts a relatively rich butterfly fauna and many diverse natural environments. Much of this diversity is a result of past geological activity, climate and geography. Thousands of years ago, the effects of continental glaciation divided the state into five physiographic regions: the Great Lakes Plain, the Till Plains, the Bluegrass or Lexington Plain, the Glaciated Allegheny Plateau and the Unglaciated Allegheny Plateau.

Historically the borders of an ancient glacial lake, the Great Lakes Plain occupies the northwestern corner of the state and is bordered to the north by Lake Erie. It represents a primarily flat strip of land that contains a variety of different habitats from extensive wetlands to scattered sandy ridges.

Sprawling across much of western Ohio, the Till Plains encompasses a large area characterized by gently rolling terrain. Scattered among existing forest were once large patches of prairie. Unfortunately, due to human land use practices, only small, remnant pockets of Ohio's prairie habitat remains today. The smallest region, located along the southern border of the state and comprising more rugged, hilly terrain is the Bluegrass or Lexington Plain. To the northeast, the topography in the Glaciated Allegheny Plateau becomes increasingly more undulating with fertile hills, rich valley forests and wetlands. Moving southeast, the Unglaciated Allegheny Plateau represents land untouched by glacial activity. Here, at the foothills of the Appalachian Mountains, terrain becomes much more rugged and local relief more extensive with dry, rocky out-crops and rich bottomland forests. The distinct topographical and soil type differences of the various regions influence the number and diversity of botanical communities present. The end result is a broad array of different habitats that support an equally diverse array of butterfly species, including some that are extremely localized and habitat restricted.

The state's climate and geography play a role as well. Although not much more than 200 miles from top to bottom, Ohio's climate varies considerably. With no mountains present to influence weather systems, the state is subject to both cold arctic air masses moving southward out of Canada and warm, moist air coming up from the Gulf of Mexico. As a result, the mean annual temperatures of northern and southern counties differ by almost 10 degrees F. Combined with its central geographical location, Ohio is at the crossroads of a wonderful mix of species' ranges, hosting those with true northern affinities as well as welcoming others with more southern tastes. As a butterfly enthusiast, it's had to ask more much more. So get outside and star enjoying the many natural riches Ohio has to offer!

WHAT ARE BUTTERFLIES?

Butterflies are insects. Along with moths, they comprise the Order Lepidoptera, a combination of Greek words meaning scale-winged, and can be differentiated from all other insects on that basis. Their four wings, as well as body, are typically almost entirely covered with numerous tiny scales. Overlapping like shingles on a roof, they make up the color and pattern of a butterfly's wings. Although generally wide and flat, some scales may be modified in shape, depending on the species and body location.

Butterflies and moths are closely related and often difficult to quickly tell apart. Nonetheless, there are some basic differences that are easy to identify even in the field. Generally, butterflies fly during the day, have large colorful wings that are held vertically together over the back when at rest, and bear distinctly clubbed antennae. In contrast, most moths are nocturnal. They are usually overall drabber in color and may often resemble dirty, hairy butterflies. At rest, they tend to hold their wings to the sides, and have feathery or threadlike antennae.

The following illustration points out the basic parts of a butterfly.

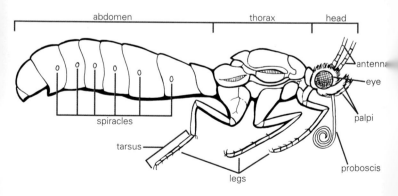

BUTTERFLY BASICS

Adult butterflies share several common characteristics, including six jointed legs, two compound eyes, two antennae, a hard exoskeleton and three main body segments: the head, thorax and abdomen.

Head

The head has two large compound eyes, two long clubbed antennae, a proboscis and two labial palpi. The rounded compound eyes are composed of hundreds of tiny individually lensed eyes. Together, they render a single, somewhat pixelated color image. Adult butterflies have good vision and are able to distinguish light in both the visible and ultraviolet range. Above the eyes are two long and slender antennae that are clubbed at the tip. They bear various sensory structures that help with orientation and smell. At the front of the head, below the eyes, are two protruding, hairy, brush-like structures called labial palpi. They serve to house and protect the proboscis, or tongue. The proboscis is a long, flexible, straw-like structure used for drinking fluids. It can be tightly coiled below the head or extended when feeding. The length of a butterfly's proboscis determines the types of flowers and other foods from which it may feed.

Thorax

Directly behind the head is the thorax. It is a large muscular portion divided into three segments that bear six legs and four wings. Each leg is jointed and contains five separate sections, the last of which is the tarsus (pl. tarsi) or foot, which bears a tiny, hooked claw at the end. In addition to enabling the butterfly to securely grasp leaves, branches or other objects, the tarsi have sensory structures that are used to taste. Adult females scratch a leaf surface with their front tarsi to release the leaf's chemicals and taste whether they have found the correct host plant. Above the legs are two pairs of wings. Made up of two thin membranes supported by rigid veins, the generally large, colorful wings are covered with millions of tiny scales that overlap like shingles on a roof. The wings serve a variety of critical functions, including flight, thermoregulation, sex recognition, camouflage, mimicry and predator deflection.

Abdomen

The last section of a butterfly's body is the long, slender abdomen. It is comprised of ten segments and contains the reproductive, digestive and excretory systems along with a series of small lateral holes, called spiracles, for air exchange. The reproductive organs or genitalia are located at the end of the abdomen. Male butterflies have two modified structures called claspers that are used to grasp the female during copulation. Females possess a genital opening for mating and a second opening for egg laying. While these structures are often difficult to see in certain species, females generally have a much larger, "fatter-looking" abdomen because they carry a large complement of eggs.

THE BUTTERFLY LIFE CYCLE

All butterflies pass through a life cycle consisting of four developmental stages: egg, larva, pupa and adult. Regardless of adult size, they begin life as a small egg. A female butterfly may lay her eggs singly, in small clusters or in large groupings on or near the appropriate host plant. Once an egg hatches, the tiny larva begins feeding almost immediately. Butterfly larvae are herbivores—with the exception of Harvester larvae, which eat aphids—and they essentially live to eat. As a result, they can grow at an astonishing rate. All insects including butterflies have an external skeleton. In order to grow, a developing caterpillar (or larva) must shed its skin, or molt, several times during its life. Each time the larva does, it discards its old, tight skin to make room for the new, roomier and often different-looking skin underneath. These different stages in a caterpillar's growth are called instars. Once fully grown, the larva stops eating and seeks a safe place to pupate. It usually attaches itself to a branch, twig or other surface with silk and molts for the last time to reveal the pupa (or chrysalis). Inside, the larval structures are broken down and reorganized into the form of an adult butterfly. At the appropriate time, the pupa splits open and a beautiful new butterfly emerges. The adult hangs quietly and begins to expand its crumpled wings by slowly forcing blood through the veins. After a few hours, its wings are fully hardened and the butterfly is ready to fly.

BUTTERFLY FAMILIES

Butterflies can be divided into five major families: Hesperiidae, Lycaenidae, Nymphalidae, Papilionidae and Pieridae. The members of each family have certain basic characteristics and behaviors that can be particularly useful for identification. Keep in mind that the features listed are only generalities, not hard and fast rules, and that there may be individual exceptions.

Hesperiidae: Skippers

Skippers are small- to medium-sized butterflies with robust, hairy bodies and relatively compact wings. They are generally brown, orange or white and their antennae bear short, distinct hooks at the tip. Adults have a quick and erratic flight, usually low to the ground. There are three main subfamilies: banded skippers, giant-skippers and spread-wing skippers.

Banded skippers (Subfamily Hesperiinae) are small brown or orange butterflies with somewhat pointed forewings. Many have dark markings or distinct black forewing stigmas. They readily visit flowers and hold their wings together over the back while feeding. Adults often perch or rest in a characteristic posture with forewings held partially open and hindwings separated and lowered further.

As their name suggests, **giant-skippers** (Subfamily Megathyminae) dwarf most other members of the family. They are medium-sized brown butterflies with yellow markings and thick, robust bodies. The adults have a fast and rapid flight. Males establish territories and generally perch on low vegetation. Adults do not visit flowers.

Spread-wing skippers (Subfamily Pyrginae) are generally dark, dull-colored butterflies with wide wings. Most have small, light spots on the forewings. Some species have hindwing tails. The adults often feed, rest and perch with their wings outstretched. They readily visit flowers.

Lycaenidae: Gossamer Wings

This diverse family includes coppers, harvesters, blues, hairstreaks and metalmarks. The adults are small and often brilliantly colored but easily overlooked. Throughout the state, blues and hairstreaks predominate, with only one harvester, two metalmarks and three coppers.

Coppers (Subfamily Lycaeninae) are small, sexually dimorphic butterflies. As their name suggests, the upper wing surfaces of most species are ornately colored with metallic reddish orange or purple. Many eastern species are associated with moist habitats including bogs, wet meadows and marshes. Populations are often quite localized but may be numerous when encountered. Adults typically scurry close to the ground with a quick flight and frequently visit available flowers or perch on low-growing vegetation with their wings held partially open.

The **harvester** (Subfamily Miletinae) is the only North American member of this unique, primarily Old World, subfamily. It is our only butterfly with carnivorous larvae. Instead of feeding on plants, the larvae devour woolly aphids. The adults do not visit flowers, but sip honeydew, a sugary secretion produced by their host aphids.

Aptly named, **blues** (Subfamily Polyommatinae) are generally bright blue on the wings above. The sexes differ and females may be brown or dark gray. The wings beneath are typically whitish gray with dark markings and distinct hindwing eyespots. The eyes are wrapped around the base of the antennae. The palpi are reduced and close to the head. Adults have a moderately quick and erratic flight, usually low to the ground. At rest, they hold their wings together over the back. Males frequently puddle at damp ground. Most blues are fond of open, disturbed sites with weedy vegetation.

Metalmarks (Subfamily Riodininae) are characterized by metallic flecks of color or even overall metallic-looking wings. They have eyes entirely separate from the antennal bases, and the palpi are quite prominent. Metalmarks reach tremendous diversity of colors and patterns in the tropics. By contrast, most U.S. species are small rust, gray or brownish butterflies. They characteristically perch with their colorful wings outstretched and may often land on the underside of leaves, especially when disturbed. Adults have a low, scurrying flight. Several species are of conservation concern.

Hairstreaks (Subfamily Theclinae) tend to be larger than blues. The wings below are often intricately patterned and bear colorful eyespots adjacent to one or two small, distinct, hair-like tails on each hindwing. The adults have a quick, erratic flight and can be a challenge to follow. They regularly visit flowers and hold their wings together over the back while feeding and at rest. Additionally, they have a unique behavior of moving their hindwings up and down when perched. The sexes regularly differ. Hairstreaks can be found in a wide range of habitats. Many species have a single spring generation.

Nymphalidae: Brush-Foots

Brush-foots are the largest and most diverse family of butterflies. In all members, the first pair of legs is significantly reduced and modified into small brush-like structures, giving the family its name and the appearance of only having four legs.

Emperors (Subfamily Apaturinae) are medium-sized and brownish with short, stubby bodies and a robust thorax. Their wings typically have dark markings and small dark eyespots. The adults are strong and rapid fliers. Males establish territories and perch on tree trunks or overhanging branches. At rest, they hold their wings together over the back. They feed on dung, carrion, rotting fruit or tree sap and do not visit flowers. Emperors inhabit rich woodlands and rarely venture far into open areas. They are nervous butterflies and difficult to closely approach.

Leafwings (Subfamily Charaxinae) are medium-sized butterflies with irregular wing margins. They are bright tawny orange above, but mottled gray to brown below and resemble a dead leaf when resting with their wings closed. The adults have a strong, rapid and erratic flight. They are nervous butterflies and difficult to closely approach. Males establish territories and perch on tree trunks or overhanging branches. Individuals also often land on the ground. They feed on dung, carrion, rotting fruit or tree sap and do not visit flowers.

Milkweed butterflies (Subfamily Danainae) are large butterflies with boldly marked black and orange wings. Their flight is strong and swift with periods of gliding. Adults are strongly attracted to flowers and feed with their wings folded tightly over the back. Males have noticeable black scent patches in the middle of each hindwing. This subfamily includes the Monarch, which undergoes massive, long-distance migrations.

Longwing butterflies (Subfamily Heliconiinae) are colorful, medium-sized butterflies. They have narrow, elongated wings, slender bodies, long antennae and large eyes. Their flight tends to be slow and fluttering. The adults readily visit flowers and nectar with their wings open. Most tend to be long-lived. Within the group are fritillaries. They are small- to medium-sized orange and black butterflies of open, sunny habitats. Those in the genus *Speyeria* have boldly patterned ventral hindwings with conspicuous metallic silver spots.

Snouts (Subfamily Libytheinae) are medium-sized, generally drab brown butterflies representing about ten species worldwide with only one found in the U.S. They have extremely elongated labial palpi and cryptically colored ventral hindwings. They rest with their wings tightly closed and resemble dead leaves.

Admirals (Subfamily Limenitidinae) are medium- to large-sized butterflies with broad, colorful wings. The adults fly with a series of quick wing beats followed by a brief period of gliding. They are typically associated with immature, secondary-growth woodlands or semi-open shrubby sites. Males perch on sunlit leaves or branches and make periodic exploratory flights. They will feed at flowers as well as rotting fruit, dung, carrion and tree sap.

True brush-foots (Subfamily Nymphalinae) are colorful, small- to medium-sized butterflies with no overall common wing shape. Most have stubby, compact bodies and a robust thorax. The adults have a strong, quick flight, usually low to the ground. Most are nervous and often difficult to approach. At rest, they hold their wings together over the back. Many are attracted to flowers while others feed on dung, carrion, rotting fruit or tree sap.

Satyrs and *wood nymphs* (Subfamily Satyrinae) are small- to medium-sized drab brown butterflies. Their wings are marked with dark stripes and prominent eyespots. The adults have a slow, somewhat bobbing flight usually low to the ground. They inhabit shady woodlands and adjacent open, grassy areas. The adults rarely visit flowers. They are instead attracted to dung, carrion, rotting fruit or tree sap. At rest, they hold their wings together over the back and are generally easy to closely approach. They regularly land on the ground.

Papilionidae: Swallowtails

Swallowtails are easily recognized by their large size and noticeably long hindwing tails. They are generally dark with bold markings. The adults have a swift and powerful flight, usually several meters off the ground, and regularly visit flowers. Most swallowtails continuously flutter their wings while feeding. Males often puddle at damp ground. They generally are found in and along woodland areas and adjacent open sites.

Pieridae: Sulphurs and Whites

Members of the family are small- to medium-sized butterflies. As their name suggests, the adults are typically some shade of white or yellow. Many have dark markings. Most species are sexually dimorphic and seasonally variable. The adults have a moderately quick and erratic flight, usually low to the ground. They are fond of flowers and hold their wings together over the back while feeding. Males often puddle at damp ground. *Sulphurs* (Subfamily Coliadinae) and *whites* (Subfamily Pierinae) are common butterflies of open, disturbed sites where their weedy larval host plants abound.

OBSERVING BUTTERFLIES IN THE FIELD

While butterflies are entertaining and beautiful to watch, correctly identifying them can often be a challenge. But it's generally not as difficult as it might seem. With a little practice and some basic guidelines, you can quickly learn to peg that unknown butterfly.

One of the first and most obvious things to note when you spot a butterfly is its size. You will discover that butterflies generally come in one of three basic dimensions: small, medium and large. This system may sound ridiculously arbitrary at first, but when you begin to regularly observe several different butterflies together in the field, these categories quickly start to make sense. For a starting point, follow this simple strategy: the next time you see a Monarch butterfly, pay close attention to its size. You may wish to use your hand as a reference. Most Monarchs have a wingspan close to the length of your palm (about four inches) as measured from the base of your fingers to the start of your wrist. This is considered a large butterfly. From here it's basically a matter of fractions. A medium-sized butterfly by comparison would have a wingspan of generally about half that size (about two inches). Finally, a butterfly would be considered small if it had a wingspan one quarter that of a Monarch (around one inch).

Next, pay close attention to color and pattern of the wings. This field guide is organized by color, and you can quickly navigate to the appropriate section. First, start by noting the overall ground color. Is it, for example, primarily black, yellow, orange or white? Then try to identify any major pattern elements such as distinct stripes, bands or spots. Depending on the behavior of the butterfly in the wild, keep in mind that the most visible portion of a butterfly may either be the upper surface of the wings (dorsal surface) or the underside (ventral surface). If you have a particularly cooperative subject, you may be able to closely observe both sides. Finally, carefully note the color and position of any major markings. For example, if the butterfly has a wide yellow band on the forewing, is it positioned in the middle of the wing or along the outer edge? Lepidopterists have a detailed vocabulary for wing pattern positions. The follow-

ing illustrations of general wing features and wing areas
should help you become familiar with some terminology.

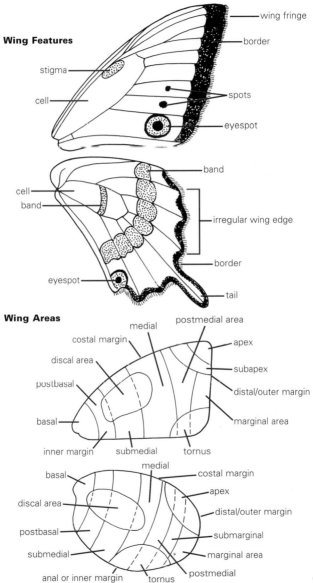

Wing Features

wing fringe

border

stigma

cell

spots

eyespot

band

cell

band

irregular wing edge

border

eyespot

tail

Wing Areas

medial

postmedial area

costal margin

apex

discal area

subapex

postbasal

distal/outer margin

basal

marginal area

inner margin

submedial

tornus

medial

basal

costal margin

discal area

apex

distal/outer margin

postbasal

submarginal

submedial

marginal area

anal or inner margin

postmedial

tornus

Next, note the shape of the butterfly's wings, particularly the forewings. Are they generally long and narrow, rounded, broad, pointed or angled? Butterflies such as the Atlantis Fritillary have noticeably elongated wings. Others, like the Carolina Satyr and Eastern Tailed-Blue, have short, generally rounded wings. Next, do the wings have any unique features? Many swallowtails and hairstreaks have distinct hindwing tails, while Question Marks and Eastern Commas have visibly irregular wing margins. Clues like this can help you quickly narrow the butterfly down to a particular family or distinguish it from a similarly colored species.

The way a butterfly flies may also be useful for identification. While it is generally difficult to easily pick up particular features or color patterns when a butterfly is moving, its flight pattern can often be very distinctive. Carefully follow the butterfly as it flies and watch how it behaves in the air. Is it soaring above your head or scurrying rapidly along the ground? Is it moving fast and erratically, or fluttering slowly about? Monarchs, for instance, have a very unique flight pattern. They flap their wings quickly several times, glide for bit, and then quickly flap their wings again. Other butterflies, such as most wood nymphs and satyrs, have a characteristic low, bobbing flight.

Sometimes you can gain important clues about a butterfly by the way it behaves when feeding. Next time you see a butterfly feeding, watch its wings. Does it hold them tightly closed, spread them wide open, or flutter them? Most swallowtails continuously flutter their wings. This behavior is a quick and reliable diagnostic that can be seen from a fair distance.

Note the habitat in which the butterfly occurs. Is it darting between branches along a shady and moist woodland path? Perched on the top of a grass blade in a saltwater marsh? Bobbing among low grasses in a wet prairie? Fluttering from one flower to the next in a fallow agricultural field? Many butterflies have strong habitat preferences. Some are restricted to a single particular habitat while others may occur in a wide range of habitats.

Sometimes even the date can offer a useful hint. Many hairstreaks are univoltine, meaning they produce just one generation. As a result, the adults occur only during a narrow window of time each spring. Similarly, several butterflies overwinter as adults. They may be active at times when few other species are around.

Butterfly observation and identification are skills, and it takes time and practice to master them. To speed up the learning curve, you may also wish to join a local butterfly gardening or watching club or society. The members can help give advice, accompany you in the field, or share directions to great butterfly watching spots.

DETERMINING A BUTTERFLY'S COLOR

To help make butterfly field identification fun and easy, this guide is organized by color, allowing you to quickly navigate to the appropriate section. In addition, smaller butterflies are always toward the beginning of each section, and the largest are toward the back. Butterflies are not static subjects, so determining their color can be a bit tricky. Several factors such as age, seasonal variation and complex wing and color patterns may affect your perception of a butterfly's color.

Age

Adult age can influence a butterfly's color. While butterflies don't get wrinkles or gray hairs, they do continue to lose wing scales during their life. This type of normal wing wear combined with more significant wing damage can cause once vibrant colors or iridescence to fade and pattern elements to become less distinct. As a result, the bright tawny orange wings of a freshly emerged Great Spangled Fritillary may appear dull orange or almost yellowish in an old, worn individual.

Seasonal Variation

Time of year can play a role as well. Some butterflies produce distinct seasonal forms that may vary significantly in color and to a lesser extent in wing shape or overall size. For the Sleepy Orange, the change is dramatic. Individuals produced during the summer are bright butter yellow on the wings below. Winter-forms, by contrast, have dark rust-colored ventral hindwings perfect for blending into a predominantly brown fall and winter landscape. For species that display extensive seasonal variation, the differences are discussed and every attempt is made to include an image of both forms. Since you'll probably be looking for butterflies in the warmer months, pictures of winter-forms are insets and not main images.

Complex Wing and Color Patterns

For many butterflies, wing color and pattern can vary tremendously between the dorsal and ventral surface. The wings of a White M Hairstreak are brilliant iridescent blue above and brownish gray below. The bright dorsal coloration is readily visible during flight but concealed at rest when the hairstreak holds its wings firmly closed. As a result, the butterfly may appear either blue or black depending on your perspective and the butterfly's activity.

Most hairstreaks (subfamily Theclinae) and sulphurs (subfamily Coliadinae) typically feed and rest with their wings closed. As a result, very few photographs of the dorsal wing surface of free-flying butterflies in these groups exist. Similarly, most blues (subfamily Polyommatinae) perch and feed with their wings closed or hold them only partially open when basking. Many of these same butterflies are also two-toned (blue on the dorsal surface, but whitish to grubby gray below; or orange on the dorsal surface, but much yellower below). But because a large number of these butterflies are so small, chances are that you'll notice them first when they fly and reveal their brighter dorsal coloration. Two-toned butterflies such as these have been placed in the color section that reflects the brighter coloration that you're most likely to notice first.

For example, if you're looking in the white section for a small butterfly with lots of bands and spots on the ventral surface, but can't find it, try the blue section. You might be looking at a perched Spring Azure, which is bright blue above but a rather nondescript brownish gray white below.

Color can vary slightly even among butterflies of the same

species. If you see a butterfly that appears to be tawny colored, but you can't find it in the orange section, try the brown section. You might be looking at a Tawny Emperor, which can be perceived as orange or brown, depending on the individual.

Finally, females are generally more drab than males of the same species. They can have less iridescent color, fewer or darker markings, and can appear overall darker or paler. For some species, such as the Diana Fritillary and Eastern Tailed-Blue, the females and males look very different and are pictured in separate color sections.

COLOR SECTION TROUBLESHOOTING

With all the variables that can impact the perception of a butterfly's color, identifying these creatures may seem daunting. Taking the time to check a color section or two is worth being able to positively identify a mystery butterfly.

Can't find it in...   Try looking in...

Black   Brown
In certain conditions, some of the dark brown butterflies, especially swallowtails and skippers, might appear black

Blue   Blue or Black
Blues (subfamily Polyommatinae) often rest or feed with their wings closed, so the blue dorsal coloration is visible primarily during flight or when the individual is basking. Check the illustration and description for field marks. Some black butterflies have varying amounts of iridescent blue scales; they may look blue in certain conditions.

Brown   Orange
Many butterflies described as tawny can be perceived as either brown or orange.

Gray   Brown
Many of the Hairstreaks (subfamily Theclinae) have light colored ventral wings that can vary in the amount of gray or brown they show.

Green   White
Some of the female Sulphurs (subfamily Coliadinae) have a common white form that may appear to be greenish.

19

Orange   Brown

Many of the skippers are brown but have bright orange field marks. Other butterflies are tawny colored, so could be perceived as either brown or orange.

White   Blue

Blues (subfamily Polyommatinae) perch with their wings closed, so appear to be white butterflies.

Yellow   Orange

Some of the Sulphurs (subfamily Coliadinae) have bright orange dorsal wings.

BUTTERFLY GARDENING

One of the easiest ways to observe local butterflies is to plant a butterfly garden. Even a small area can attract a great variety of species directly to your yard. For best results, include both adult nectar sources and larval host plants. Most adult butterflies are generalists and will visit a broad range of colorful flowers in search of nectar. Developing larvae, on the other hand, typically have very discriminating tastes and often rely on only a few very specific plant species for food. For assistance with starting a butterfly garden, seek the guidance of local nursery professionals. They can help you determine which plants will grow well in your area. This field guide provides a list of larval host plants for each species, as well as a listing of good nectar plants. These lists begin on page 334.

BUTTERFLY Q & A:
What's the difference between a butterfly and a moth?

While there is no one simple answer to this question, butterflies and moths generally differ based on their overall habits and structure. Butterflies are typically active during the day (diurnal), while moths predominantly fly at night (nocturnal). Butterflies possess slender antennae that are clubbed at the end. Those of moths vary from long narrow filaments to broad fern-like structures. At rest, butterflies tend to hold their wings together vertically over the back. Moths rest with their wings extended flat out to the sides or folded alongside the body. Butterflies generally have long, smooth and slender bodies. The bodies of moths are often robust and hairy. Finally, most butterflies are typically brightly colored, while most moths tend to be dark and somewhat drab.

What can butterflies see?

Butterflies are believed to have very good vision and to see a single color image. Compared to humans, they have an expanded range of sensitivity and are able to distinguish wavelengths of light into the ultraviolet range.

Do butterflies look the same year-round?

Many butterflies produce distinct seasonal forms that differ markedly in color, size, reproductive activity and behavior. Good examples within Ohio include the Common Buckeye and Sleepy Orange. The seasonal forms are determined by the environmental cues (temperature, rainfall, day length) that immature stages experience during development. Warm summer temperatures and long days forecast conditions that are highly favorable for continued development and reproduction. Summer-form individuals are generally lighter in color, short-lived, and reproductively active. As fall approaches, cooler temperatures and shortening day lengths mean future conditions may be unfavorable for continued development and reproduction. Winter-form adults display increased pattern elements, are generally darker, larger, longer lived, and survive the winter months in a state of reproductive diapause.

Do caterpillars have eyes?

Yes, caterpillars or larvae generally have six pairs of simple eyes called ocelli. They are able to distinguish basic changes in light intensity but are believed to be incapable of forming an image.

How do caterpillars defend themselves?

Caterpillars or larvae are generally plump, slow moving creatures that represent an inviting meal for many predators. To protect themselves, caterpillars employ a variety of different strategies. Many, like the Monarch or Pipevine Swallowtail, sequester specific chemicals from their host plants that render them highly distasteful or toxic. These caterpillars are generally brightly colored to advertise their unpalatability. Others rely on deception or camouflage to avoid being eaten. White Admiral larvae are mottled green, brown and cream, a color pattern that helps them resemble a bird dropping. By contrast, larvae of the Northern Pearly Eye are solid green and extremely well camouflaged against the green leaves of their host. Some larvae conceal their whereabouts by constructing shelters. American Painted Lady larvae weave leaves and flowerheads together with silk and rest safely inside when not actively feeding. Still others have formidable spines and hairs or produce irritating or foul-smelling chemicals to deter persistent predators.

Do butterfly caterpillars make silk?

Yes, butterfly larvae produce silk. While they don't typically spin an elaborate cocoon around their pupa like moths, they use silk for a variety of purposes, including the construction of shelters, anchoring or attaching their chrysalid, and to gain secure footing on leaves and branches.

What happens when a butterfly's scales rub off?

Contrary to the old wives' tale, if you touch a butterfly's wing and remove scales in the process it is still capable of flying. In fact, a butterfly typically continuously loses scales during its life from normal wing wear. Scales serve a variety of purposes, from thermoregulation and camouflage to pheromone dispersal and species or sex recognition, but are not critical for flight. Once gone, the scales are permanently lost and will not grow back.

Why do butterflies gather at mud puddles?

Adult butterflies are often attracted to damp or moist ground and may congregate at such areas in large numbers. In most cases, these groupings, or "puddle clubs," are made up entirely of males. They drink from the moisture to gain water and salts (sodium ions) that happen to come into solution. This behavior helps males replenish the sodium ions lost when they pass a packet of sperm and accessory gland secretions to the female during copulation. The transferred nutrients have been shown to play a significant role in egg production and, thus, female reproductive output.

How long do butterflies live?

In general, most butterflies are extremely short-lived and survive in the wild for an average of about two weeks. There are, of course, numerous exceptions to this rule. The Mourning Cloak is a perfect example. Adults may survive for 4–6 months. Still others, particularly species that migrate long distances and/or overwinter as adults, are capable of surviving for extended periods of time.

Where do butterflies go at night?
Where do they go during a rainstorm?

In the evening or during periods of inclement weather, most butterflies seek shelter under the leaves of growing plants or among vegetation.

Do all butterflies visit flowers?

All butterflies are fluid feeders. While a large percentage of them rely on sugar-rich nectar as the primary energy source for flight, reproduction and general maintenance, many species also feed on, or exclusively utilize, the liquids and dissolved nutrients produced by other food resources such as dung, carrion, rotting fruit or vegetation, sap and bird droppings.

Do butterflies grow?

No. An adult butterfly is fully grown upon emergence from its chrysalis.

How do caterpillars grow?

A caterpillar's job in life is to eat and grow. But larvae, like all other insects, have an external skeleton. Therefore, in order to increase in size, they must shed their skin, or molt, several times during development. Essentially, their skin is like a trash bag. It is packed full of food until there is no more room. Once full, it is discarded for a larger, baggier one underneath and the process continues.

What eats butterflies?

Butterflies face an uphill battle for survival. Out of every one hundred eggs produced by a female butterfly, approximately only one percent survive to become an adult. And as an adult, the odds don't get much better. Various birds, small mammals, lizards, frogs, toads, spiders and other insects all prey on butterflies.

What's the difference between a chrysalis and a cocoon?

Once fully grown, both moth and butterfly caterpillars molt a final time to form a pupa. Most moths surround their pupae with a constructed silken case called a cocoon. By contrast, a butterfly pupa, frequently termed a chrysalis, is generally naked. In most cases, butterfly chrysalid are attached to a leaf, twig or other surface with silk. In some instances, they may be unattached or surrounded by a loose silken cocoon.

Are all butterfly scales the same?

No. The scales on a butterfly's wings and body come in a variety of different sizes and shapes. Some may be extremely elongated and resemble hairs while others are highly modified for the release of pheromones during courtship. Those responsible for making up wing color and pattern are generally wide and flat. They are attached at the base and overlap like shingles on a roof. The colors we see are the result of either pigments contained in the scales or the diffraction of light caused by scale structure. Iridescent colors such as blue, green, purple and silver usually result from scale structure. While pigmented scales are the norm, many species have a combination of both types on their wings.

BUTTERFLY QUICK-COMPARE

Common Sootywing
pg. 41

Grizzled Skipper
pg. 43

Baltimore Checkerspot
pg. 45

Red Admiral
pg. 47

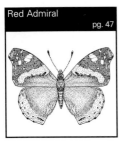

Milbert's Tortoiseshell
pg. 49

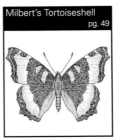

White Admiral
pg. 51

Zebra Swallowtail
pg. 53

Black Swallowtail
pg. 55

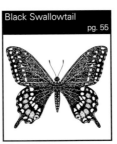

Pipevine Swallowtail
pg. 57

Mourning Cloak
pg. 59

Red-spotted Purple
pg. 61

Diana Fritillary
pg. 63

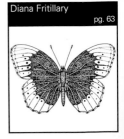

Spicebush Swallowtail
pg. 65

Eastern Tiger Swallowtail
pg. 67

Eastern Tailed-Blue
pg. 69

Reakirt's Blue
pg. 71

Spring Azure
pg. 73

Summer Azure
pg. 75

Silvery Blue
pg. 77

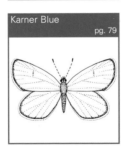

Karner Blue
pg. 79

Appalachian Azure
pg. 81

White M Hairstreak
pg. 83

Eastern Tailed-Blue
pg. 85

Reakirt's Blue
pg. 87

Brown Elfin pg. 89	Frosted Elfin pg. 91	Swarthy Skipper pg. 93
	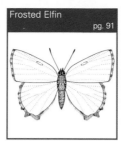	

Tawny-edged Skipper pg. 95	Eastern Pine Elfin pg. 97	Henry's Elfin pg. 99

Pepper and Salt Skipper pg. 101	Coral Hairstreak pg. 103	Purplish Copper pg. 105
	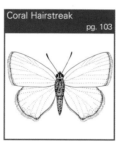	

Banded Hairstreak pg. 107	Edwards' Hairstreak pg. 109	Hickory Hairstreak pg. 111
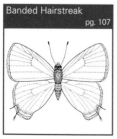		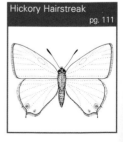

Crossline Skipper
pg. 113

Peck's Skipper
pg. 115

Southern Hairstreak
pg. 117

Striped Hairstreak
pg. 119

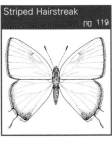

Common Roadside-Skipper
pg. 121

Mulberry Wing
pg. 123

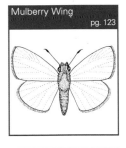

Hayhurst's Scallopwing
pg. 125

Zabulon Skipper
pg. 127

Northern Broken-Dash
pg. 129

Little Glassywing
pg. 131

Sachem
pg. 133

Carolina Satyr
pg. 135

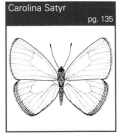

Cobweb Skipper
pg. 137

Dun Skipper
pg. 139

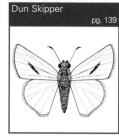

Acadian Hairstreak
pg. 141

Dreamy Duskywing
pg. 143

Two-spotted Skipper
pg. 145

Confused Cloudywing
pg. 147

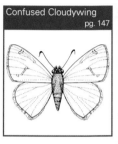

Southern Cloudywing
pg. 149

Columbine Duskywing
pg. 151

Mottled Duskywing
pg. 153

Black Dash
pg. 155

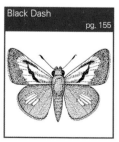

Northern Cloudywing
pg. 157

Bronze Copper
pg. 159

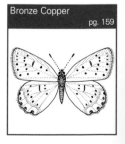

Gemmed Satyr
pg. 161

Persius Duskywing
pg. 163

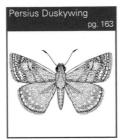

Hobomok Skipper
pg. 165

Horace's Duskywing
pg. 167

Wild Indigo Duskywing
pg. 169

Sleepy Duskywing
pg. 171

Mitchell's Satyr
pg. 173

Dusted Skipper
pg. 175

Hoary Edge
pg. 177

Leonard's Skipper
pg. 179

Ocola Skipper
pg. 181

Juvenal's Duskywing
pg. 183

Little Wood Satyr
pg. 185

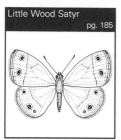

Golden-banded Skipper
pg. 187

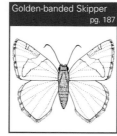

American Snout
pg. 189

Eyed Brown
pg. 191

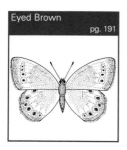

Appalachian Brown
pg. 193

Silver-spotted Skipper
pg. 195

Common Buckeye
pg. 197

Northern Pearly Eye
pg. 199

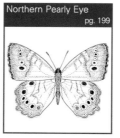

Hackberry Butterfly
pg. 201

Common Wood Nymph
pg. 203

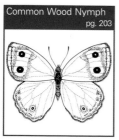

Tawny Emperor
pg. 205

Compton Tortoiseshell
pg. 207

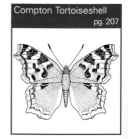

Giant Swallowtail
pg. 209

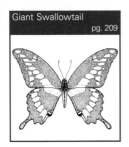

Red-banded Hairstreak
pg. 211

Dusky Azure
pg. 213

Gray Hairstreak
pg. 215

Acadian Hairstreak
pg. 217

Early Hairstreak
pg. 219

Juniper Hairstreak
pg. 221

Least Skipper
pg. 223

European Skipper
pg. 225

Northern Metalmark
pg. 227

Swamp Metalmark
pg. 229

Purplish Copper
pg. 231

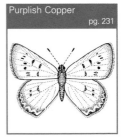

Long Dash
pg. 233

Fiery Skipper
pg. 235

American Copper
pg. 237

Harvester
pg. 239

Delaware Skipper
pg. 241

Zabulon Skipper
pg. 243

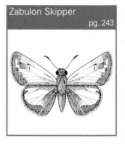

Sachem
pg. 245

Indian Skipper
pg. 247

Pearl Crescent
pg. 249

Black Dash
pg. 251

Bronze Copper
pg. 253

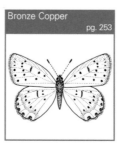

Hobomok Skipper
pg. 255

Dion Skipper
pg. 257

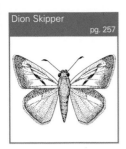

Meadow Fritillary
pg. 259

Duke's Skipper
pg. 261

Sleepy Orange
pg. 263

Harris's Checkerspot
pg. 265

Silvery Checkerspot
pg. 267

Northern Crescent
pg. 269

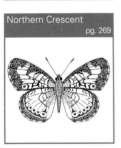

Broad-winged Skipper
pg. 271

Silver-bordered Fritillary
pg. 273

Variegated Fritillary
pg. 275

Orange Sulphur
pg. 277

Painted Lady
pg. 279

American Painted Lady
pg. 281

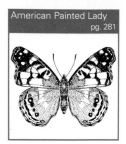

Eastern Comma
pg. 283

Gray Comma
pg. 285

Atlantis Fritillary
pg. 287

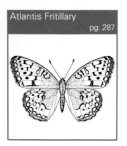

Goatweed Butterfly
pg. 289

Question Mark
pg. 291

Viceroy
pg. 293

Aphrodite Fritillary
pg. 295

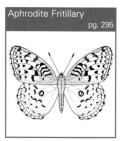

Great Spangled Fritillary
pg. 297

Regal Fritillary
pg. 299

Monarch
pg. 301

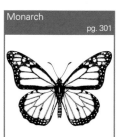

Diana Fritillary
pg. 303

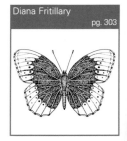

Common/White Checkered-Skipper pg. 305	West Virginia White pg. 307	Olympia Marble pg. 309
	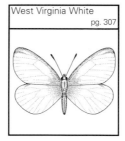	

Falcate Orangetip pg. 311	Checkered White pg. 313	Cabbage White pg. 315
	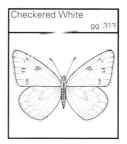	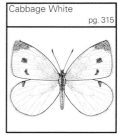

Clouded Sulphur pg. 317	Zebra Swallowtail pg. 319	Dainty Sulphur pg. 321
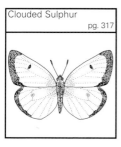		

Little Sulphur pg. 323	Southern Dogface pg. 325	Clouded Sulphur pg. 327
		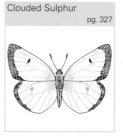

Cloudless Sulphur

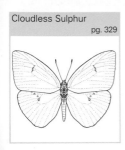

Eastern Tiger Swallowtail

Common Name
Scientific Name

color section indicators →

Family/Subfamily: tells which family and subfamily the butterfly belongs to (see p. 9–13 for descriptions)

Wingspan: gives minimum and maximum wing spans, from one forewing tip to the other

Above: description of upper, or dorsal, surface of wings

Below: description of lower, or ventral, surface of wings

Sexes: describes differences in appearance between male and female

Egg: description of eggs and where they are deposited

Larva: description of the butterfly's larva, or caterpillar

Larval Host Plants: lists plants that eggs and larva are likely to be found on

Habitat: describes where you're likely to find the butterflies

Broods: lists number of broods, or generations, hatched in a span of one year

Abundance: when the butterflies are flying, this tells you how often you're likely to encounter them

Compare: describes differences among similar-looking species

range map shows where in Ohio this butterfly is present

Resident: predictably present
Visitor: occasionally present
Stray: rarely present

phenogram: shows population flux throughout the year

Resident Visitor Stray

Jan. Feb. Mar. Apr. May June July Aug. Sept. Oct. Nov. Dec.

Dorsal (above)

silhouette behind Comments section shows actual average size of butterfly

Ventral (below)

illustration shows field marks and features to look for

39

Ventral

Larva

Comments: The Common Sootywing indeed looks as if
it fell into a pail of ashes. The silky blackish brown
wings of fresh individuals are particularly lovely when
seen in full sun. Tolerant of human disturbance, it is at
home in a variety of open, weedy sites that support its
naturalized host. The butterfly is avidly drawn to available flowers as well as damp soil. Adults have a low,
erratic flight and frequently perch on low vegetation or
bare soil with their wings spread. The larvae construct
individual shelters on the host by folding over part of a
leaf with silk.

Common Sootywing
Pholisora catullus

Family/Subfamily: Skippers (Hesperiidae)/
Spread-wing Skippers (Pyrginae)

Wingspan: 0.90–1.25" (2.3–3.2 cm)

Above: shiny dark brown to black with a variable number
of small white spots on the forewing and a few on top
of the head

Below: as above but paler brown

Sexes: similar, although female often has larger white
forewing spots

Egg: reddish pink, laid singly on upperside of host leaves

Larva: pale gray-green with a narrow dorsal stripe, pale
green lateral stripes, a black collar and black head;
body is covered with numerous tiny yellow-white dots,
each bearing a short hair

Larval Host Plants: primarily Lamb's Quarters,
Mexican Tea and Spiny Amaranth

Habitat: open, disturbed sites including roadsides, old
fields, utility easements and fallow agricultural land

Broods: two or more generations

Abundance: occasional to common

Compare: Hayhurst's Scallopwing (pg. 125) has distinctly scalloped hindwing margins and tends to prefer
more shaded habitats.

Resident

Jan.	Feb.	Mar.	Apr.	May	June	July	Aug.	Sept.	Oct.	Nov.	Dec.

male

Dorsal (above)
small white spots
otherwise black

white spots on head

occasionally has a row
of small white spots
on hindwing

Ventral (below)
blackish brown

Ventral

Larva

Comments: This primarily Canadian butterfly is found in portions of the central Appalachians and Upper Midwest where it is considered rare and declining. In Ohio, it is now listed as endangered and is reported from only one location. Superficially similar to the more widespread and abundant Common Checkered-Skipper, the Grizzled Skipper appears noticeably darker. Adults scurry with a very quick, somewhat bouncing flight close to the ground. They periodically perch on low vegetation or in sunlit patches on bare earth with their wings held open. Both sexes are fond of flowers and readily visit available blossoms.

Grizzled Skipper
Pyrgus centaureae

Family/Subfamily: Skippers (Hesperiidae)/
Spread-wing Skippers (Pyrginae)

Wingspan: 1.1–1.3" (2.8–3.3 cm)

Above: dark gray to black with scattered small, white
spots and black-and-white checkered fringes; forewing
has scattered white spots; central band is missing a
white spot below cell-end bar

Below: white with irregular olive gray bands and spots

Sexes: similar

Egg: pale green, laid singly on the underside of host
leaves

Larva: gray green with a black head

Larval Host Plants: Canada Cinquefoil

Habitat: open oak woodlands, barrens, forest clearings
and margins, utility easements and along forest trails

Broods: single generation

Abundance: rare; localized

Compare: Common/White Checkered-Skipper (pg. 305)
is larger and has more extensive white spotting.

Resident

Jan. Feb. Mar. Apr. May June July Aug. Sept. Oct. Nov. Dec.

Dorsal (above)
scattered small white
spots

missing white spot
below cell

checkered fringes

Ventral (below)
irregular bands and
spots

43

Ventral

Larva

Comments: With its outrageously colored pattern, the Baltimore is truly a must-see butterfly! Unfortunately, like many other wetland species, it continues to decline as a result of habitat loss or alteration. It primarily occurs in habitat-restricted populations that tend to be highly fragmented and localized but occasionally quite abundant. Females lay their eggs on Turtlehead. Upon hatching, the young larvae construct a communal silken web on the plant and feed gregariously inside until the end of summer. The partially grown larvae overwinter and resume development in the following spring on potential alternate hosts.

Baltimore Checkerspot
Euphydryas phaeton

Family/Subfamily: Brush-foots (Nymphalidae)/
True Brush-foots (Nymphalinae)

Wingspan: 1.75–2.50" (4.4–6.6 cm)

Above: black with reddish orange spots along the outer
wing margins and several rows of cream white spots

Below: marked as above with several large reddish
orange basal spots on both wings

Sexes: similar

Egg: yellow, soon turning reddish, laid in large clusters of
several hundred on the underside of host leaves

Larva: tawny orange with black transverse stripe and
several rows of black, branched spines; front and rear
end segments are black

Larval Host Plants: Turtlehead is the primary host;
secondary hosts include a wider range of plants such
as false foxglove, Narrowleaf Plantain, Canadian
Lousewort, and Southern Arrowwood

Habitat: wet meadows, fens, bogs, stream margins,
marshes and moist fields

Broods: single generation

Abundance: uncommon; localized

Compare: unique

Resident

Jan. Feb. Mar. Apr. May June July Aug. Sept. Oct. Nov. Dec.

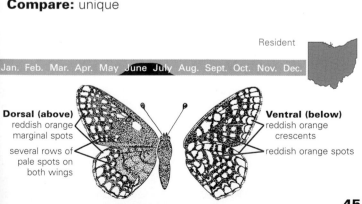

Dorsal (above)
reddish orange
marginal spots

several rows of
pale spots on
both wings

Ventral (below)
reddish orange
crescents

reddish orange spots

45

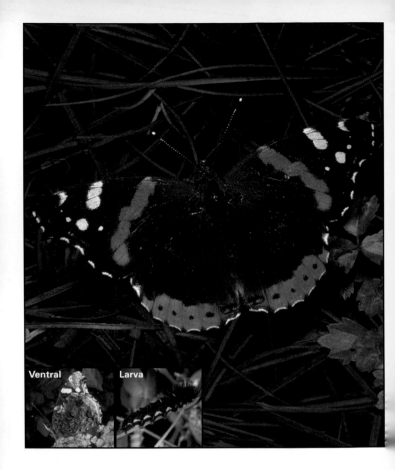

Ventral Larva

Comments: The Red Admiral is quickly distinguished
from all other butterflies by its distinctive reddish
orange forewing band. Particularly common in early
summer, it prefers rich woodland edges and other
moist places near patches of its host but will readily
explore nearby habitats and may be a frequent garden
visitor. It occasionally experiences tremendous population outbreaks. In southern Ohio, adults sometimes
survive the winter. Males frequently perch on low vegetation, or on the ground in sunlit locations. Adults
occasionally nectar at flowers but more frequently visit
sap flows, dung or fermenting fruit.

Red Admiral
Vanessa atalanta

Family/Subfamily: Brush-foots (Nymphalidae)/
True Brush-foots (Nymphalinae)

Wingspan: 1.75–2.50" (4.4–6.4 cm)

Above: dark brownish black with reddish orange hind-wing border and distinct, reddish orange median forewing band; forewing has small white spots near apex

Below: forewing as above with blue scaling and paler markings; hindwing ornately mottled with dark brown, blue and cream in bark-like pattern

Sexes: similar

Egg: small green eggs laid singly on host leaves

Larva: variable; pinkish gray to charcoal with lateral row of cream crescent-shaped spots and numerous branched spines. Larvae construct individual shelters on the host by folding together one or more leaves with silk.

Larval Host Plants: False Nettle, Pellitory and nettles

Habitat: moist woodlands, forest edges, roadside ditches, canals and pond margins, wetlands, parks, meadows and gardens

Broods: two or more generations

Abundance: occasional to common; locally abundant

Compare: unique

Visitor

| Jan. | Feb. | Mar. | Apr. | May | June | July | Aug. | Sept. | Oct. | Nov. | Dec. |

Dorsal (above)
forewing apex
squared off
white spots
reddish orange
band

Ventral (below)
pale apex
reddish orange band

Ventral

Larva

Comments: This small but electric tortoiseshell has to be seen in person to be truly appreciated. Particularly common in the Upper Midwest, Milbert's Tortoiseshell reaches the southernmost extension of its eastern range around central Ohio but occasionally wanders well beyond the state's boundaries. It is rare south of Columbus. Unlike other anglewings, the species regularly visits a variety of flowers for nectar in addition to feeding at fermenting fruit, dung, carrion and sap flows. Males frequently perch on fallen logs or bare earth to await passing females. They tend to be quite wary and dart off with a rapid, low flight if disturbed.

Milbert's Tortoiseshell
Nymphalis milberti

Family/Subfamily: Brush-foots (Nymphalidae)/
True Brush-foots (Nymphalinae)

Wingspan: 1.9–2.4" (4.8–6.1 cm)

Above: two-toned; basal portion is velvety chocolate
brown with reddish orange bars in the forewing cell,
outer portion has dark wing margins bordered inwardly
with a wide yellow orange band; hindwing border
encloses a row of small blue spots; forewing apex is
extended and squared off; hindwing bears a single
short, stubby tail

Below: strongly two-toned; basal half dark blackish
brown and outer portion grayish brown with fine striations and a dark border; resembles tree bark

Sexes: similar

Egg: green, laid in clusters on host leaves

Larva: black with two pale lateral bands, white speckling,
and several rows of branched, black spines; the ventral
surface is gray green

Larval Host Plants: Stinging Nettle

Habitat: wet meadows, stream margins, pastures and
other open areas near moist woodlands

Broods: two generations

Abundance: rare to occasional

Compare: unique

Resident

Jan. Feb. Mar. Apr. May June July Aug. Sept. Oct. Nov. Dec.

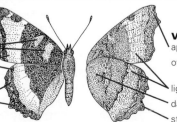

Dorsal (above)
two orange bars
outer third of
wings yellow
orange
small blue spots
in border

Ventral (below)
apex squared off
overall bark-like
pattern
lighter band
dark basal half
stubby tail

49

Ventral   Larva

Comments: This distinctive butterfly of northern forests essentially replaces the Red-spotted Purple throughout much of the Upper Midwest, Northeast and Canada. Although not a resident of Ohio, the White Admiral readily hybridizes with the Red-spotted Purple in areas where their ranges overlap. Numerous intergradations more closely resembling the White Admiral may occasionally be encountered in northern Ohio. Adults have a strong, gliding flight and are often quite wary. Males regularly perch on sunlit leaves or on gravel roads and make periodic exploratory flights. Both sexes will visit flowers but prefer rotting fruit, dung, carrion or tree sap.

White Admiral
Limenitis arthemis arthemis

Family/Subfamily: Brush-foots (Nymphalidae)/ Admirals (Limenitidinae)

Wingspan: 3.0–3.5" (7.6–8.9 cm)

Above: dark velvety bluish black with a broad white band across both wings; hindwing has a submarginal row of orange spots and iridescent blue dashes along the margin

Below: brownish black with a broad white band, reddish orange basal spots and a row of reddish orange spots along the outer portion of both wings

Sexes: similar

Egg: gray-green, laid singly on host leaves

Larva: mottled green, brown and cream with two long, knobby horns on the thorax; resembles a bird dropping. Young larvae eat the tip of the leaf to the mid-vein and rest on the end of the vein when not actively feeding.

Larval Host Plants: birches, poplars and aspens

Habitat: open woodlands, forest clearings, wooded roadsides and adjacent open areas

Broods: one to two broods where resident

Abundance: rare

Compare: Red-spotted Purple (pg 61) lacks the broad white bands.

Visitor

| Jan. | Feb. | Mar. | Apr. | May | June | July | Aug. | Sept. | Oct. | Nov. | Dec. |

Dorsal (above)
wide, white postmedian band
submarginal blue spot band
red spot band

Ventral (below)
wide, white postmedian band
reddish brown

51

Ventral

Larva

Comments: Easily our most elegant species, the long-tailed black-and-white-striped Zebra Swallowtail can be confused with no other resident butterfly. Adults have a low, rapid flight and adeptly maneuver through the understory or among shrubby vegetation. Seldom found far from stands of its larval host, it is unlikely to be encountered in highly developed areas although may occasionally wander into nearby home gardens in search of nectar. The swallowtail has a proportionately short proboscis and is thus unable to feed at many long, tubular flowers. It instead prefers composites, and is regularly attracted to white flowers.

Zebra Swallowtail
Eurytides marcellus

Family/Subfamily: Swallowtails (Papilionidae)/ Swallowtails (Papilioninae)

Wingspan: 2.5–4.0" (6.4–10.2 cm)

Above: white with black stripes and long, slender tails; hindwings bear a bright red patch above the eyespot; spring-forms are smaller, lighter and have shorter tails

Below: as above, but with a red stripe through hindwing

Sexes: similar

Egg: light green, laid singly on host leaves or budding branches

Larva: several color forms; may be green, green with light blue and yellow stripes or charcoal with white and yellow stripes

Larval Host Plants: pawpaw

Habitat: open deciduous woodlands, stream corridors, old fields, forest edges and roads

Broods: multiple generations

Abundance: occasional to common

Compare: unique

Resident

Jan. Feb. Mar. Apr. May June July Aug. Sept. Oct. Nov. Dec.

male

Dorsal (above)
pale greenish white and black stripes

red spot

long black tails edged in white

Ventral (below)
red stripe

53

Male

Female

Ventral

Larva

Comments: The Black Swallowtail is one of our most common garden butterflies. Its plump, green larvae, often referred to as "parsley worms," feed on many cultivated herbs and may occasionally become minor nuisance pests. It is equally at home in undisturbed wetlands and rural meadows as in suburban yards and urban parks. Males have a strong, rapid flight and frequently perch on vegetation or actively patrol open areas for females. Both sexes are exceedingly fond of flowers and stop to nectar at available blossoms. It is one of five Ohio butterflies that mimic the toxic Pipevine Swallowtail to gain protection from predators.

Black Swallowtail
Papilio polyxenes

Family/Subfamily: Swallowtails (Papilionidae)/
Swallowtails (Papilioninae)

Wingspan: 2.5–4.2" (6.4–10.7 cm)

Above: male is black with a broad, postmedian yellow
band and a row of marginal yellow spots; female is
mostly black with increased blue hindwing scaling and
marginal yellow spots, the yellow postmedian band is
reduced; both sexes have a red hindwing eyespot with
a central black pupil, and a yellow-spotted abdomen

Below: hindwing has orange-tinted yellow spot bands

Sexes: dissimilar; female has reduced yellow postmedian
band and increased blue hindwing scaling above

Egg: yellow, laid singly on host leaves

Larva: green with black bands and yellow-orange spots

Larval Host Plants: wild and cultivated members of
the carrot family including Queen Anne's Lace, angelica, wild parsnip, dill, fennel and parsley

Habitat: old fields, roadsides, pastures, weedy sites,
suburban gardens, marshes, agricultural land, vacant
lots, prairies, open woodlands and utility corridors

Broods: multiple generations

Abundance: occasional to abundant

Compare: Spicebush Swallowtail (pg. 65) is larger and
has green-blue submarginal spots.

Resident

Jan. Feb. Mar. Apr. May June July Aug. Sept. Oct. Nov. Dec.

male

Dorsal (above)
yellow bands
blue scaling
black "pupil" in
center of spot
tail

Ventral (below)
yellow-orange bands
faint yellow-orange
cell spot

55

Male

Ventral

Larva

Comments: The Pipevine Swallowtail's prominent black wings and orange ventral marking help showcase its unpalatable nature. During development, the fleshy larvae sequester various toxins from their pipevine hosts, rendering them and the resulting adults highly distasteful to certain predators. As a result, five other butterflies in Ohio mimic its color pattern to help them gain protection. Common through southern Ohio, the Pipevine Swallowtail becomes more scarce northward. Adults have a rapid, low flight but are fond of colorful flowers. They rarely linger at any one blossom for long, tending to be rather wary and nervous of approach.

Pipevine Swallowtail
Battus philenor

Family/Subfamily: Swallowtails (Papilionidae)/ Swallowtails (Papilioninae)

Wingspan: 2.75–4.00" (7.0–10.2 cm)

Above: overall black; male has iridescent greenish blue hindwings; female is duller black with a single row of white marginal spots

Below: hindwings are iridescent blue with a row of prominent orange spots

Sexes: dissimilar; female is dull black with a more prominent row of white spots

Egg: brownish orange, laid singly or in small clusters

Larva: velvety black with orange spots and numerous fleshy tubercles

Larval Host Plants: various pipevines, including Woolly Pipevine, Dutchman's Pipe and Virginia Snakeroot

Habitat: fields, pastures, roadsides, open woodlands, stream corridors, suburban gardens

Broods: multiple generations

Abundance: rare to common

Compare: Spicebush Swallowtail (pg. 65) is larger with prominent crescent-shaped marginal spots. Red-Spotted Purple (pg. 61) lacks hindwing tails. Female Black Swallowtail (pg. 55) is larger with an orange hindwing eyespot.

Resident

| Jan. | Feb. | Mar. | Apr. | May | June | July | Aug. | Sept. | Oct. | Nov. | Dec. |

male

Dorsal (above)
black forewings
idescent green-blue
row of pale spots

Ventral (below)
large orange spots
iridescent blue

57

Ventral

Larva

Comments: This rich beauty of a butterfly is the first har-
binger of spring; overwintering adults occasionally
become active on warm winter days and fly about even
with snow still on the ground. It produces only a single
generation each year. Adults emerge in early summer,
aestivate until fall, become active again to feed and
build up fat reserves before seeking protected sites to
hibernate—making it one of our longest lived butterflies. Although widespread and often fairly common, it
is typically encountered in very small numbers or as
solitary individuals. Adults seldom visits flowers but are
frequently seen at rotting fruit or sap flows.

Mourning Cloak
Nymphalis antiopa

Family/Subfamily: Brush-foots (Nymphalidae)/ True Brush-foots (Nymphalinae)

Wingspan: 3.0–4.0" (7.6–10.2 cm)

Above: velvety black, often appearing iridescent, with broad irregular yellow border and a row of bright purple blue spots; forewing apex is extended and squared off; hindwing bears a single short, stubby tail

Below: silky black with pale wing border, heavily striated and bark-like in appearance

Sexes: similar

Egg: light brown, laid in clusters on host leaves or twigs

Larva: black with a dorsal row of crimson patches, fine white speckling and several rows of black, branched spines

Larval Host Plants: birch, willow, aspen, elm and hackberry

Habitat: deciduous forests, clearings, riparian woodlands, woodland roads, forest edges, wetland and watercourse margins, and adjacent open areas including suburban yards, parks and golf courses

Broods: single generation

Abundance: uncommon to occasional

Compare: unique

Resident

Jan. Feb. Mar. Apr. May June July Aug. Sept. Oct. Nov. Dec.

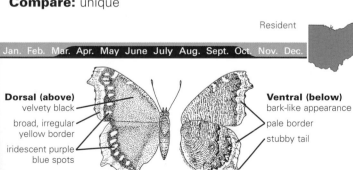

Dorsal (above)
velvety black

broad, irregular yellow border

iridescent purple blue spots

Ventral (below)
bark-like appearance

pale border

stubby tail

Ventral   Larva

Comments: The Red-spotted Purple is one of several Ohio butterflies that mimic the toxic Pipevine Swallowtail to gain protection from predators such as birds. It is a common butterfly of immature woodlands, but is rarely encountered in large numbers. Adults have a strong, gliding flight and are often quite wary. Males perch on sunlit leaves along trails or forest margins and make periodic exploratory flights. Adults occasionally visit flowers but often prefer rotting fruit, dung, carrion or tree sap.

Red-Spotted Purple
Limenitis arthemis astyanax

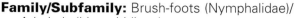

Family/Subfamily: Brush-foots (Nymphalidae)/ Admirals (Limenitidinae)

Wingspan: 3.0–4.0" (7.6–10.2 cm)

Above: dark velvety bluish black with iridescent blue scaling on hindwing and small orange and white spots near forewing apex

Below: brownish black with an iridescent blue sheen and basal red-orange spots; hindwings have a row of red-orange spots toward the outer margin

Sexes: similar

Egg: gray-green, laid singly on the tips of host leaves

Larva: mottled green, brown and cream with two long, knobby horns on thorax; resembles a bird dropping

Larval Host Plants: Black Cherry, Wild Cherry and willow

Habitat: open deciduous woodlands, forest edges and adjacent open areas

Broods: two generations

Abundance: occasional to common

Compare: Pipevine Swallowtail (pg. 57) has hindwing tail and a low, rapid flight; continually flutters wings when nectaring. Spicebush Swallowtail (pg. 65) has submarginal row of pale green spots and a hindwing tail.

Resident

Jan. Feb. Mar. Apr. May June July Aug. Sept. Oct. Nov. Dec.

Dorsal (above)
iridescent blue
hindwing is squared off

Ventral (below)
pale forewing apex
red-orange spots

Female

Male pg. 303

Male

Larva

Comments: The Diana Fritillary is primarily restricted to the moist, deciduous forests throughout the Appalachian Mountains from West Virginia to Mississippi. Although historically found within the state, urban development and related human land use practices have eliminated much of its previously available habitat, resulting in extirpation of the species.

Diana Fritillary
Speyeria diana

Family/Subfamily: Brush-foots (Nymphalidae)/ Longwing Butterflies (Heliconiinae)

Wingspan: 3.5–4.4" (8.9–11.2 cm)

Above: male is dark unmarked blackish brown with bright orange on the outer third; female is black basally with white and iridescent blue spots on outer half

Below: forewing is orange with heavy black markings toward base; male hindwing is brownish orange with two rows of small narrow silver dashes; female hindwing is chocolate brown

Sexes: dissimilar; female is black basally with white and iridescent blue spots on outer half; ventral hindwing is chocolate brown

Egg: tiny cream eggs laid singly and somewhat haphazardly near host leaves

Larva: velvety black with several rows of reddish orange based black spines

Larval Host Plants: various woodland violets

Habitat: rich, moist deciduous mountain woodlands, stream corridors, forested roads, clearings and adjacent open areas

Broods: single generation

Abundance: extirpated

Compare: unique

No longer present

Jan. Feb. Mar. Apr. May June July Aug. Sept. Oct. Nov. Dec.

male

Dorsal (above)
black
orange
(male primarily black and blue)

Ventral (below)
black markings toward base

lacks prominent silvery hindwing spots characteristic of other fritillaries

63

Male

Ventral

Larva

Comments: The lovely Spicebush Swallowtail is one of five Ohio butterflies that mimic the unpalatable Pipevine Swallowtail to gain protection from predators. Adults are strong, agile fliers that rarely stray far from their preferred habitats and are unlikely to be found in highly urban areas. Although recorded in every county, it tends to be considerably more common in southern Ohio. A true lover of flowers, the adults nectar at available wildflowers and may be frequent garden visitors. The brightly colored larvae make individual shelters on the host by curling up both edges of a leaf with silk. They rest motionless inside when not actively feeding.

Spicebush Swallowtail
Papilio troilus

Family/Subfamily: Swallowtails (Papilionidae)/ Swallowtails (Papilioninae)

Wingspan: 3.5–5.0" (8.9–12.7 cm)

Above: black with a row of large, pale greenish blue spots along the margin; hindwings have greenish blue scaling and a single, orange eyespot

Below: black with postmedian band of blue scaling bordered by row of yellow-orange spots on each side; abdomen black with longitudinal rows of light spots

Sexes: similar, female has duller hindwing scaling

Egg: cream, laid singly on the underside of host leaves

Larva: green above, reddish below with enlarged thorax, two false eyespots and several longitudinal rows of blue spots

Larval Host Plants: Sassafras and Spicebush

Habitat: deciduous forests, woodland margins, pastures, old fields, forested roadsides and suburban gardens

Broods: multiple generations

Abundance: occasional

Compare: Pipevine Swallowtail (pg. 57), female Black Swallowtail (pg. 55) and dark-form female Eastern Tiger Swallowtail (pg. 67) all lack marginal greenish blue spots.

Resident

Jan. Feb. Mar. Apr. May June July Aug. Sept. Oct. Nov. Dec.

Dorsal (above)
orange spot
large pale green spots
iridescent green-blue patch
spoon-shaped tails

Ventral (below)
yellow-orange spots
blue scaling

65

Dark-form female

Dark-form female

Female

Male pg. 331

Female

Larva

Comments: Easily recognized by its bold, black stripes and bright yellow wings, the Eastern Tiger Swallowtail is spectacular in pattern and size. Adults have a strong, agile flight and often soar high in the treetops. Although fond of woodlands and waterways, it is equally at home in more urban areas and is a conspicuous garden visitor. Unlike many other swallowtails, the adults seldom flutter their wings while feeding. They instead rest on the blossom with their colorful wings outstretched. Dark-form females mimic the toxic Pipevine Swallowtail to gain protection from predators. Males often congregate at moist earth or animal dung.

Eastern Tiger Swallowtail
Papilio glaucus

Family/Subfamily: Swallowtails (Papilionidae)/ Swallowtails (Papilioninae)

Wingspan: 3.5–5.5" (8.9–14.0 cm)

Above: yellow with black forewing stripes and broad black wing margins; single row of yellow spots along outer edge of each wing

Below: yellow with black stripes and black wing margins; hindwing margins have increased blue scaling and a single submarginal row of yellow-orange, crescent-shaped spots; abdomen yellow with black stripes

Sexes: dissimilar; male always yellow but females have two color forms; yellow female has increased blue scaling in black hindwing border; dark-form female is mostly black with extensive blue hindwing markings

Egg: green, laid singly on upper surface of host leaves

Larva: green; enlarged thorax and two small false eyespots

Larval Host Plants: Wild Cherry, Black Cherry, ash and Tulip Tree

Habitat: deciduous forests, woodland margins, gardens, parks, old fields, pastures, roadsides, alfalfa fields

Broods: multiple generations

Abundance: occasional to common

Compare: Pipevine Swallowtail (pg. 57) is much smaller. Spicebush Swallowtail (pg. 65) has greenish-blue spots on hindwing margin.

Resident

Jan. Feb. Mar. Apr. May June July Aug. Sept. Oct. Nov. Dec.

male

Dorsal (above)
yellow with black stripes

wide black border

yellow spots

long tail

Ventral (below)
yellow-orange spots

blue scaling

Male

Female pg. 85

Ventral

Larva

Comments: The Eastern Tailed-Blue is widespread and common throughout most of the eastern United States and one of our most abundant species. Named for its distinctive hindwing tail, it is the only blue in Ohio with this characteristic hairstreak-like feature. Do not rely solely on the presence of tails for identification, as they are fragile and may often be lost with normal wing wear. Adults have a weak, dancing flight. They are fond of flowers and easily attracted to the garden. Males often gather in small puddle clubs at damp sand or gravel. Rests and feeds with wings closed, so blue color shows in flight or while basking.

Eastern Tailed-Blue
Everes comyntas

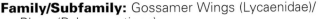

Family/Subfamily: Gossamer Wings (Lycaenidae)/ Blues (Polyommatinae)

Wingspan: 0.75–1.00" (1.9–2.5 cm)

Above: male is blue with brown border; female is brownish gray; both sexes have one or two small orange and black hindwing spots above single tail

Below: silvery gray with numerous dark spots and bands; hindwing has two small orange-capped black spots above tail

Sexes: dissimilar; female is primarily brownish gray

Egg: pale green, laid singly on flowers or young leaves of host

Larva: variable, typically green with dark dorsal stripe and light lateral stripes

Larval Host Plants: wide variety of herbaceous Fabaceae including clover, bush clover, Alfalfa, sweet clover and beggarweeds

Habitat: open, disturbed sites including roadsides, vacant lots, old fields, utility easements, fallow agricultural land, pastures, prairies and home gardens

Broods: multiple generations

Abundance: occasional to common; locally abundant

Compare: Summer Azure (pg. 75) lacks tails and orange spot along hindwing margin.

Resident

Jan. Feb. Mar. Apr. May June July Aug. Sept. Oct. Nov. Dec.

male

Dorsal (above)
bright blue

one or two orange-capped black spots

tail

Ventral (below)
black spots and bars outlined in white

one or two orange-capped black spots

Female pg. 87

Larva

Comments: This small southwestern resident regularly
expands its range northward into the central U.S. each
year, occasionally establishing temporary breeding
colonies or wandering as far north as the Canadian
border. It is unable to survive harsh winter conditions.
Nonetheless, Reakirt's Blue is a rare vagrant to Ohio. It
is primarily a butterfly of weedy, disturbed sites but
could be encountered in virtually any open habitat. It
typically rests and feeds with its wings closed; blue
color is seen primarily in flight or while the butterfly is
basking.

Reakirt's Blue
Hemiargus isola

Family/Subfamily: Gossamer Wings (Lycaenidae)/ Blues (Polyommatinae)

Wingspan: 0.75–1.10" (1.9–2.8 cm)

Above: male is light blue with a narrow brown border; female is primarily dark gray-brown with reduced blue scaling limited to the wing bases. Both sexes have a prominent small black marginal spot along the outer edge of the hindwing.

Below: light gray with numerous white bands and dark spots; forewing has a distinct postmedian row of white-rimmed round black spots

Sexes: dissimilar; female is primarily dark gray-brown with reduced blue scaling

Egg: greenish blue, laid singly on flower buds of host

Larva: pinkish red with lateral white stripes. The larvae are regularly tended by ants.

Larval Host Plants: wide variety of plants in the bean family including mesquite, acacia, sweet clover, prairie clover, Alfalfa, White Clover and scarlet-pea

Habitat: potentially any open habitat

Broods: multiple generations

Abundance: rare

Compare: Silvery Blue (pg. 77) has a submarginal row of round black spots on the wings below.

Stray

Jan. Feb. Mar. Apr. May June July Aug. Sept. Oct. Nov. Dec.

male

Dorsal (above)
purplish blue
small black spots

Ventral (below)
forewing apex sharply cut off
prominent round black spots
gray

71

Male

Larva

Comments: The Spring Azure is by far the most abundant and noticeable early-season blue in Ohio, often seen even before many of the colorful spring flowering trees and shrubs are in full bloom. A butterfly of deciduous forests and associated trails or margins, it may occasionally wander into nearby open areas including suburban yards. Adults have a moderately slow flight and erratically scurry from ground level to canopy height, moving just over the surface of the vegetation. They are extremely fond of flowers and often congregate at damp ground. Rests and feeds with wings closed, so blue color shows in flight or while basking.

Spring Azure
Celastrina ladon

Family/Subfamily: Gossamer Wings (Lycaenidae)/
Blues (Polyommatinae)

Wingspan: 0.75–1.25" (2.0–3.2 cm)

Above: male is pale blue with narrow, faint dark
forewing border; lacks white scaling on wings

Below: somewhat variable; dusky gray with black spots
and dark scaling along hindwing margin and often a
dark patch in the center of the hindwing

Sexes: dissimilar; female has a broader, more extensive
dark forewing border above

Egg: whitish green; laid singly on flower buds of host

Larva: variable; green to pinkish green to whitish with
dark dorsal stripe and cream bands

Larval Host Plants: flowers of various trees and
shrubs including Black Cherry, blueberry, Flowering
Dogwood, Gray Dogwood and viburnum

Habitat: open, deciduous woodlands, forest edges and
trails, roadsides, brushy fields, utility easements,
wooded swamps and gardens

Broods: single generation

Abundance: occasional to common

Compare: All other azures are silver gray on the wings
below with reduced dark markings.

Resident

Jan. Feb. Mar. Apr. May June July Aug. Sept. Oct. Nov. Dec.

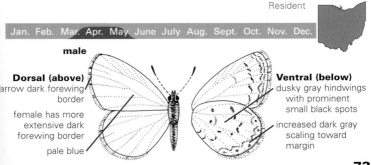

male

Dorsal (above)
narrow dark forewing
border

female has more
extensive dark
forewing border

pale blue

Ventral (below)
dusky gray hindwings
with prominent
small black spots

increased dark gray
scaling toward
margin

73

Male | Female | Larva

Comments: Although now viewed as a distinct species, the Summer Azure was previously considered a lighter, second generation form of the similar, early-season Spring Azure. Adults of this small dusty blue butterfly are found in and along woodlands but readily venture out into nearby open areas in search of nectar and may frequently wander into suburban yards and gardens. They have a moderately slow, dancing flight and unlike most other blues are often encountered fluttering high among the branches of trees and shrubs. Males often congregate at damp ground. Blue color shows in flight or while basking.

Summer Azure
Celastrina neglecta

Family/Subfamily: Gossamer Wings (Lycaenidae)/ Blues (Polyommatinae)

Wingspan: 0.80–1.25" (2.0–3.2 cm)

Above: male is light blue with narrow, faint dark border on forewing and increased white scaling on hindwing

Below: chalky white with small dark spots and bands

Sexes: dissimilar, female has increased white scaling above and wide, dark forewing borders

Egg: whitish green, laid singly on flower buds of host

Larva: variable; green to pinkish green with dark dorsal stripe and cream bands

Larval Host Plants: flowers of various trees and shrubs (occasionally herbaceous plants) including New Jersey Tea, Wing-stem, holly and sumac

Habitat: open, deciduous woodlands, forest edges and trails, stream margins, roadsides, brushy fields, utility easements, wooded swamps and gardens

Broods: two or more generations

Abundance: occasional to common

Compare: Spring Azure (pg. 73) is duskier gray and more heavily marked below; the wings above lack white scaling. Appalachian Azure (pg. 81) is slightly larger and has a reduced row of dark spots along the ventral hindwing margin.

Resident

Jan.	Feb.	Mar.	Apr.	May	June	July	Aug.	Sept.	Oct.	Nov.	Dec.

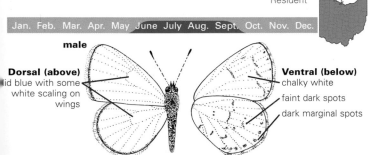

male

Dorsal (above)
lid blue with some white scaling on wings

Ventral (below)
chalky white
faint dark spots
dark marginal spots

75

Male   Larva

Comments: The Silvery Blue is one of our most beautiful
spring butterflies. Although wide-ranging across much
of Canada and the western U.S., Ohio populations are
part of a separate Appalachian Mountain group that
extends from Pennsylvania into northern Georgia. It is
often encountered alongside several of the early-season azures. It typically occurs in low-density, isolated
colonies, seldom far from stands of its larval hosts.
Adults have a low, quick and often directed flight but
frequently stop to nectar at small spring flowers and
are particularly fond of their host blossoms. Males
often gather at mud puddles to imbibe moisture.

Silvery Blue
Glaucopsyche lygdamus

Family/Subfamily: Gossamer Wings (Lycaenidae)/ Blues (Polyommatinae)

Wingspan: 1.00–1.25" (2.5–3.2 cm)

Above: male is uniform bright metallic silvery blue with narrow black wing borders and a white fringe

Below: light brownish gray with a prominent row of white-rimmed round black spots across the wings

Sexes: dissimilar; female is charcoal gray with dusky metallic blue overscaling and broad dark wing borders

Egg: pale blue-green, laid singly young shoots, new leaves or flower buds of host

Larva: gray green with a dark green dorsal stripe and white, oblique dashes; turns reddish prior to pupation

Larval Host Plants: Carolina Vetch and possibly other legumes

Habitat: moist openings or clearings in deciduous woodlands, utility corridors, forested roads and brushy fields

Broods: single generation

Abundance: rare to occasional; localized

Compare: Reakirt's Blue (pg. 71) is lavender-blue above and lacks the distinct postmedian row of white-rimmed black spots on the hindwing below.

Resident

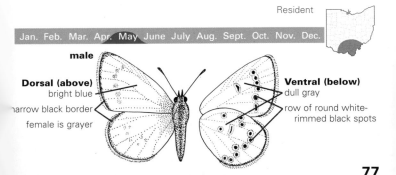

Jan. Feb. Mar. Apr. May June July Aug. Sept. Oct. Nov. Dec.

male

Dorsal (above)
bright blue
narrow black border
female is grayer

Ventral (below)
dull gray
row of round white-rimmed black spots

Male

Female

Comments: Once found from New Hampshire to Minnesota, the Karner Blue's geographic distribution and population numbers have been severely reduced as a result of urban development, expanding agriculture and fire suppression. Today, the butterfly is critically imperiled, being restricted to small, isolated pockets of remnant habitat and listed as both a state and federal endangered species. Once extirpated, a successful breeding population has been reestablished at one site in Ohio. Additional sites are being planned by the Ohio Karner Blue Recovery team led by the Division of Wildlife and the Toledo Zoological Gardens.

Karner Blue
Lycaeides melissa samuelis

Family/Subfamily: Gossamer Wings (Lycaenidae)/ Blues (Polyommatinae)

Wingspan: 1.00–1.35" (2.5–304 cm)

Above: male is bright blue with a narrow black border and white wing fringe; female has reduced blue scaling and broad brown margins; hindwing has a marginal row of small, orange-capped black spots

Below: whitish gray with numerous small, white-rimmed black spots and a distinctive orange submarginal spot band

Sexes: dissimilar; female has reduced blue scaling and marginal row of orange-capped black spots on the hindwing

Egg: light greenish, laid singly on or near the host

Larva: light green; tended by ants

Larval Host Plants: Wild Lupine

Habitat: openings in oak savannas or barrens

Broods: two generations

Abundance: rare; localized

Compare: unique; the distinct orange submarginal band on the wings below distinguish it from all other blues in the state.

No longer present

| Jan. | Feb. | Mar. | Apr. | May | June | July | Aug. | Sept. | Oct. | Nov. | Dec. |

male

Dorsal (above)
continuous black line

bright blue

Ventral (below)
red-orange submarginal band outlined by black spots

79

Larva

Comments: The Appalachian Azure is our largest resident blue. As its name suggests, it is restricted to moist, deciduous forests of the Appalachians. Its single spring generation is seldom on the wing for more than a few weeks. It appears to be temporally isolated from other azures, flying after the peak of the Spring Azure and just before the emergence of the Summer Azure. It is generally rather uncommon, occurring in small, isolated and low-density colonies close to its sole larval host. Males often gather in numbers at mud puddles along stream banks or unpaved woodland roads. Blue color shows while basking or in flight.

Appalachian Azure
Celastrina neglectamajor

Family/Subfamily: Gossamer Wings (Lycaenidae)/ Blues (Polyommatinae)

Wingspan: 1.1–1.4" (2.8–3.6 cm)

Above: male is uniform light blue with a narrow dark forewing border; lacks extensive white scaling

Below: chalky white with very pale, small dark spots; hindwing has faint zigzag band along margin enclosing an incomplete row of one to three prominent dark spots

Sexes: dissimilar; female has broad dark wing borders

Egg: pale green, laid singly (although often several on each plant) on flower buds of host

Larva: variable; yellow green to reddish brown with an often incomplete dark dorsal band and faint or absent oblique cream dashes

Larval Host Plants: flowers of Black Cohosh

Habitat: moist, cool shaded woodlands, forest trails, woodland roads and stream corridors

Broods: single generation

Abundance: rare to uncommon; localized

Compare: Summer Azure (pg. 75) is smaller and has increased white scaling on dorsal hindwing, but may not reliably be separated in the field.

Resident

Jan. Feb. Mar. Apr. May June July Aug. Sept. Oct. Nov. Dec.

male

Dorsal (above)
narrow dark border
light blue

Ventral (below)
pale chalky white
incomplete row of faint dark spots

81

Female

Larva

Comments: A large butterfly compared to most members of the family, the White M Hairstreak is named for the narrow white band on the ventral hindwing that forms a distinct letter M or W, depending on your perspective. The true beauty of this diminutive species can be seen mainly during flight, when the bright iridescent blue scaling of the upper wing surfaces flash in the sunlight. Unfortunately, it is seldom seen in Ohio and can be considered a "good find." At home along oak woodlands and moist forest borders, adults readily explore open adjacent areas for flowers. Adults have a quick, erratic flight and can be difficult to follow.

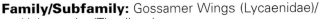

White M Hairstreak
Parrhasius m-album

Family/Subfamily: Gossamer Wings (Lycaenidae)/ Hairstreaks (Theclinae)

Wingspan: 1.0–1.5" (2.5–3.8 cm)

Above: male is bright iridescent blue with broad, black margins and two hindwing tails; female is dull black with blue scaling limited to wing bases

Below: brownish gray; hindwing has a single red eyespot above tail, white spot along leading margin, and a narrow white line forming a distinct M in middle of wing

Sexes: dissimilar; female duller with blue basal scaling

Egg: whitish, laid singly on twigs or buds of host

Larva: variable, dark green to mauve

Larval Host Plants: American Basswood and various oaks including White Oak

Habitat: open woodlands, forest margins and adjacent, roadsides, utility easements, and old fields

Broods: two generations

Abundance: rare

Compare: Southern Hairstreak (pg. 117) lacks the prominent single red spot inward from the tails and the white spot along the leading margin of the ventral hindwing; wings above are brown.

Resident

| Jan. | Feb. | Mar. | Apr. | May | June | July | Aug. | Sept. | Oct. | Nov. | Dec. |

male

Dorsal (above)
iridescent blue
wide black borders

Ventral (below)
white spot
white M
red spot
blue patch

Female

Male pg. 69   Ventral   Larva

Comments: The Eastern Tailed-Blue is widespread and common throughout most of the eastern United States and one of our most abundant species. Named for its distinctive hindwing tail, it is the only blue in Ohio with this characteristic hairstreak-like feature. Do not rely solely on the presence of tails for identification, as they are fragile and may often be lost with normal wing wear. Adults have a weak, dancing flight. They are fond of flowers and easily attracted to the garden. Males often gather in small puddle clubs at damp sand or gravel.

Eastern Tailed-Blue
Everes comyntas

Family/Subfamily: Gossamer Wings (Lycaenidae)/ Blues (Polyommatinae)

Wingspan: 0.75–1.00" (1.9–2.5 cm)

Above: male is blue with brown border; female is brownish gray; both sexes have one or two small orange and black hindwing spots above single tail

Below: silvery gray with numerous dark spots and bands; hindwing has two small orange-capped black spots above tail

Sexes: dissimilar; female is primarily brownish gray

Egg: pale green, laid singly on flowers or young leaves of host

Larva: variable, typically green with dark dorsal stripe and light lateral stripes

Larval Host Plants: A wide variety of herbaceous Fabaceae including clover, bush clover, Alfalfa, sweet clover and beggarweeds

Habitat: open, disturbed sites including roadsides, vacant lots, old fields, utility easements, fallow agricultural land, pastures, prairies and home gardens

Broods: multiple generations

Abundance: occasional to common

Compare: Summer Azure (pg. 75) lacks tails and orange spot along hindwing margin.

Resident

Jan. Feb. Mar. Apr. May June July Aug. Sept. Oct. Nov. Dec.

male

Dorsal (above)
bright blue

one or two orange-capped black spots

tail

Ventral (below)
black spots and bars outlined in white

one or two orange-capped black spots

Female

Male pg. 71

Larva

Comments: This small southwestern resident regularly expands its range northward into the central U.S. each year, occasionally establishing temporary breeding colonies or wandering as far north as the Canadian border. It is unable to survive harsh winter conditions. Nonetheless, Reakirt's Blue is a rare vagrant to Ohio. It is primarily a butterfly of weedy, disturbed sites but could be encountered in virtually any open habitat.

Reakirt's Blue
Hemiargus isola

Family/Subfamily: Gossamer Wings (Lycaenidae)/ Blues (Polyommatinae)

Wingspan: 0.75–1.10" (1.9–2.8 cm)

Above: male is light blue with a narrow brown border; female is primarily dark gray-brown with reduced blue scaling limited to the wing bases. Both sexes have a prominent small black marginal spot along the outer edge of the hindwing.

Below: light gray with numerous white bands and dark spots; forewing has a distinct postmedian row of white-rimmed round black spots

Sexes: dissimilar; female is primarily dark gray-brown with reduced blue scaling

Egg: greenish blue, laid singly on flower buds of host

Larva: pinkish red with lateral white stripes. The larvae are regularly tended by ants.

Larval Host Plants: wide variety of plants in the bean family including mesquite, acacia, sweet clover, prairie clover, Alfalfa, White Clover and scarlet-pea

Habitat: potentially any open habitat

Broods: multiple generations

Abundance: rare

Compare: Silvery Blue (pg. 77) has a submarginal row of round black spots on the wings below.

Stray

Jan. Feb. Mar. Apr. May June July Aug. Sept. Oct. Nov. Dec.

male

Dorsal (above)
purplish blue
small black spots

Ventral (below)
forewing apex sharply cut off
prominent round black spots
gray

87

Larva

Comments: The Brown Elfin is a delicate, tailless species of early spring. Found in close association with stands of its larval host, within Ohio it is known from only one metapopulation and may need state protection. Small size and dull brown color make individuals easy to overlook. Despite its widespread eastern range, it is primarily restricted to southern Ohio. The adults generally remain close to the ground, often pausing to perch on the ends of bare twigs, low vegetation or on bare soil. If disturbed, they rapidly dart off but travel only a short distance before alighting once more. They nectar a variety of early-season flowers.

Brown Elfin
Callophrys augustinus

Family/Subfamily: Gossamer Wings (Lycaenidae)/ Hairstreaks (Theclinae)

Wingspan: 0.8–1.1" (2.0–2.8 cm)

Above: dark brown; male has dark forewing stigma

Below: forewing brown; hindwing dark brown at base with outer portion lighter reddish brown to mahogany

Sexes: similar

Egg: whitish, laid singly host flower buds

Larva: yellow green with pale yellow oblique dorsal dashes and a yellow lateral stripe

Larval Host Plants: primarily plants in the heath family including Black Huckleberry, Leatherleaf, Highbush Blueberry, Blue Ridge Blueberry and Mountain Laurel

Habitat: open woodlands, forest margins, wooded road-sides, utility easements and possibly bogs

Broods: single generation

Abundance: rare; localized

Compare: Eastern Pine Elfin (pg. 97) has strongly patterned hindwings with numerous dark bands outlined in white. Frosted Elfin's (pg. 91) hindwing has extensive frosting and a short, stubby tail. Henry's Elfin (pg. 99) has some white on outer portion of dark basal hindwing patch, frosting along margin of hindwing and a short, stubby tail.

Resident

| Jan. | Feb. | Mar. | Apr. | May | June | July | Aug. | Sept. | Oct. | Nov. | Dec. |

Dorsal (above)
brown wings
lobed anal angle of hindwing

Ventral (below)
hindwing much darker at base
reddish brown toward outer margin

Larva

Comments: Living up to its name, the Frosted Elfin has
extensive whitish gray scaling along the outer portion
of its ventral hindwing, making it appear as if it were
dusted lightly with powdered sugar. The butterfly is
closely associated with dry openings in oak savannas
that support lupine. Rare and extremely restricted
within the state, it is found in only a few remaining
small and isolated populations. As a result, it is currently listed by the Ohio Department of Natural
Resources as endangered. It has been raised and
introduced along with the Karner Blue by the Toledo
Zoological Gardens.

Frosted Elfin
Callophrys irus

Family/Subfamily: Gossamer Wings (Lycaenidae)/ Hairstreaks (Theclinae)

Wingspan: 0.8–1.1" (2.0–2.8 cm)

Above: unmarked dark brown; male has dark forewing stigma

Below: forewing brown; hindwing dark brown at wing base, outer portion somewhat lighter with extensive gray frosting along outer margin; frosted area contains a distinct single black spot near the short, stubby tail

Sexes: similar, although female lacks forewing stigma

Egg: whitish, laid singly host flower buds

Larva: blue-green with pale white oblique dorsal dashes and a pale white lateral stripe

Larval Host Plants: Wild Lupine

Habitat: openings in oak savannas and forest margins

Broods: single generation

Abundance: rare; localized

Compare: Eastern Pine Elfin (pg. 97) has strongly patterned hindwings with numerous dark bands outlined in white. Henry's Elfin (pg. 99) lacks black spot near short, stubby tail. Brown Elfin (pg. 89) lacks hindwing frosting and short, stubby tail.

Resident

Jan.	Feb.	Mar.	Apr.	May	June	July	Aug.	Sept.	Oct.	Nov.	Dec.

Dorsal (above)
dark stigma
marked dark brown wings
short, stubby tail

Ventral (below)
irregular white line
extensive gray frosting
black spot above tail

Dorsal   Larva

Comments: This drab brown butterfly is distinctively plain and can be reliably identified on that basis. However, its small size and uneventful appearance make it an easy butterfly to quickly overlook. Although noticeable on the wing, a keen eye is needed to spot individuals resting among surrounding vegetation. Frequently encountered in dry, disturbed sites, colonies may be somewhat small and localized near host patches. Adults have a rapid and low flight. Males perch on the tops of grasses and nervously spring into motion before alighting moments later.

Swarthy Skipper
Nastra lherminier

Family/Subfamily: Skippers (Hesperiidae)/
Banded Skippers (Hesperiinae)

Wingspan: 0.9–1.1" (2.3–2.8 cm)

Above: dull dark brown, occasionally with small faint
forewing spots

Below: olive brown to yellow brown with light veins

Sexes: similar

Egg: white, laid singly on host leaves

Larva: elongate; pale green with a darker green dorsal
stripe, a pale lateral stripe and a reddish brown head
marked with vertical cream bands

Larval Host Plants: Little Bluestem and Kentucky
Bluegrass

Habitat: old fields, roadsides, woodland openings, dry
meadows and other disturbed areas

Broods: two generations

Abundance: uncommon

Compare: unique

Resident

Jan. Feb. Mar. Apr. May June July Aug. Sept. Oct. Nov. Dec.

Dorsal (above)
wings dark brown
ometimes has pale
spots

Ventral (below)
lighter veins
olive brown to yellow
brown

93

Male

Male   Larva

Comments: As its name suggests, the Tawny-edged Skipper has distinct bright orange scaling along the costal margin of the forewing that is visible from both the dorsal and ventral surfaces. Superficially quite similar to the Crossline Skipper, close observation is often required for a definitive field identification. The species prefers open grassy areas and is readily drawn to available wildflowers. Adults have a low, rapid flight and often alight on bare soil or low vegetation.

Tawny-edged Skipper
Polites themistocles

Family/Subfamily: Skippers (Hesperiidae)/
Banded Skippers (Hesperiinae)

Wingspan: 0.8–1.2" (2.0–3.0 cm)

Above: male is dark brown with prominent black stigma
and tawny orange scaling along forewing costa;
female is dark brown with small yellow spots across
forewing and reduced orange along costal margin

Below: light brown to olive brown with distinct contrasting orange scaling along costal margin of forewing

Sexes: dissimilar; female darker with reduced orange coloration

Egg: greenish white, laid singly on host leaves

Larva: reddish brown with dark dorsal stripe and black
head

Larval Host Plants: various grasses including panic
grass, Slender Crabgrass, mannagrass and bluegrass

Habitat: stream corridors, wet meadows, old fields, pastures, prairies, roadsides and suburban yards

Broods: two generations

Abundance: occasional to abundant

Compare: Crossline Skipper (pg. 113) is larger, and usually has a faint band of small, pale spots through the
center of the yellow-brown ventral hindwing. Tolerates
drier habitats.

Resident

Jan. Feb. Mar. Apr. May June July Aug. Sept. Oct. Nov. Dec.

male

Dorsal (above)
orange along costal
margin

ntinuous black stigma

Ventral (below)
orange scaling along
costal margin

unmarked olive to
brassy brown
hindwing

95

Larva

Comments: With its boldly patterned hindwings, this beautiful little spring species is our most distinctive elfin. Inhabiting a variety of open and semi-open landscapes that support stands of hard pines, the butterfly is found in close association with younger trees. Rarely encountered in any number, populations tend to be small and highly localized. Adults spend much of their time perched on host branches, often high above the ground, but frequently venture down to nectar at nearby blossoms or sip moisture at damp soil.

Eastern Pine Elfin
Callophrys niphon

Family/Subfamily: Gossamer Wings (Lycaenidae)/ Hairstreaks (Theclinae)

Wingspan: 0.80–1.25" (2.0–3.2 cm)

Above: unmarked dark brown; male has a pale gray forewing stigma

Below: brown, strongly banded with black, reddish brown and gray; hindwing has gray marginal band

Sexes: similar, although female is tawnier above and lacks pale forewing stigma

Egg: pale green, laid singly at the base of host needles

Larva: bright green with cream longitudinal stripes

Larval Host Plants: various hard pines including Virginia Pine, Loblolly Pine, Pitch Pine and Shortleaf Pine; also Eastern White Pine

Habitat: open woodlands, pine forests, woodland clearings, open, brushy fields, roadsides and utility easements

Broods: single generation

Abundance: rare to uncommon

Compare: All other elfins lack the strongly patterned ventral hindwing.

Resident

Jan. Feb. Mar. Apr. May June July Aug. Sept. Oct. Nov. Dec.

male

Dorsal (above)
pale gray stigma

tailless

Ventral (below)
banded with black, reddish brown and gray

gray marginal band

Larva (green)

Larva (red)

Comments: This is our most frequently encountered elfin. This early spring species is found in variety of wooded or semi-open areas in close association with stands of its larval hosts. As a result, the butterfly tends to be spotty and rather local but can be quite common when encountered. Population numbers often vary considerably from year to year. Adults have a quick, erratic flight and regularly perch on the tips of small tree branches or on low, shrubby vegetation. Seldom having to search far for nectar, they frequently visit available host blossoms. They may occasionally be encountered sipping moisture at damp earth.

Henry's Elfin
Callophrys henrici

Family/Subfamily: Gossamer Wings (Lycaenidae)/ Hairstreaks (Theclinae)

Wingspan: 0.9–1.2" (2.3–3.0 cm)

Above: brown with amber scaling along hindwing margin; hindwing has short, stubby tail

Below: brown; hindwing distinctly two-toned with dark brown basal half and light brown outer half; gray frosting along outer margin

Sexes: similar

Egg: whitish, laid singly on host twigs or flower buds

Larva: variable; green to reddish with oblique white dorsal markings

Larval Host Plants: primarily Redbud

Habitat: deciduous woodlands, forest edges and clearings, shrubby areas, old fields and roadsides

Broods: single spring generation

Abundance: occasional to common; localized

Compare: Eastern Pine Elfin (pg. 97) has strongly patterned ventral hindwing with numerous dark bands outlined in white. Frosted Elfin (pg. 91) has more frosting on hindwing and small dark spot near tail. Brown Elfin (pg. 89) lacks tail and gray frosting.

Resident

Jan. Feb. Mar. Apr. May June July Aug. Sept. Oct. Nov. Dec.

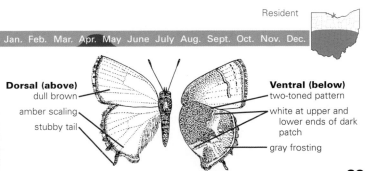

Dorsal (above)
dull brown
amber scaling
stubby tail

Ventral (below)
two-toned pattern
white at upper and lower ends of dark patch
gray frosting

99

Dorsal

Larva

Comments: Well named, this distinctive skipper does indeed look as if it were sprinkled with salt and pepper. Although widespread throughout the East, it tends to be a universally uncommon butterfly. It is most often encountered individually or in small numbers darting in and out of sunlit woodland openings or along forested roadways. The small adults speed along near the ground with a rapid and somewhat erratic flight. Males often imbibe moisture and other nutrients at damp earth.

Pepper and Salt Skipper
Amblyscirtes hegon

Family/Subfamily: Skippers (Hesperiidae)/
Banded Skippers (Hesperiinae)

Wingspan: 0.9–1.2" (2.3–3.0 cm)

Above: dark brown with checkered fringes and a band of small white spots on the forewing

Below: variable; hindwing is greenish gray with cream spot band; wing fringes are strongly checkered

Sexes: similar

Egg: light green, laid singly on host leaves

Larva: whitish green with a dark green dorsal line, a paler green subdorsal line and a reddish brown head with a pale brown crescent on each side

Larval Host Plants: various grasses including Fowl Mannagrass, Indian Grass, Kentucky Bluegrass and Indian Woodoats

Habitat: sunlit forest clearings, woodland margins, glades, stream corridors and adjacent fields

Broods: single generation

Abundance: rare to uncommon; localized

Compare: Common Roadside-Skipper (pg. 121) lacks the heavy gray overscaling and cream postmedian spot band on the ventral hindwing.

Resident

| Jan. | Feb. | Mar. | Apr. | May | June | July | Aug. | Sept. | Oct. | Nov. | Dec. |

Dorsal (above)
white spots
brown

Ventral (below)
cream spot band
hindwing frosted with light greenish gray
strongly checkered fringes

101

Male

Female

Larva

Comments: This distinctive tailless hairstreak is unlikely
to be confused with any other small butterfly on Ohio.
It frequents a variety of semi-open, brushy habitats in
close association with its somewhat aggressive,
thicket-forming hosts. Although widespread, the Coral
Hairstreak is often quite local in occurrence and is seldom encountered in large numbers. Adults have a
quick, erratic flight and readily perch on the top of
small trees or shrubs. Both sexes frequently visit flowers and are exceedingly fond of milkweed blossoms.

Coral Hairstreak
Satyrium titus

Family/Subfamily: Gossamer Wings (Lycaenidae)/ Hairstreaks (Theclinae)

Wingspan: 0.90–1.25" (2.3–3.2 cm)

Above: unmarked brown; male has a small gray forewing stigma and somewhat triangular wings

Below: light gray brown with a row of small, white-rimmed black spots across both wings and a second row of larger bright coral spots along the hindwing margin; tailless

Sexes: similar, although female has more rounded wings and lacks forewing stigma

Egg: cream, laid singly on host twigs, low on the trunks of small host trees or occasionally on leaf litter below the host

Larva: yellow green with pinkish red patches on each end

Larval Host Plants: Black Cherry, Wild Cherry and American Plum

Habitat: overgrown fields near forest margins, brushy woodland clearings, shrubby roadsides and trails, and unmanaged pastures or fencerows

Broods: single generation

Abundance: occasional to common

Compare: unique

Resident

Jan. Feb. Mar. Apr. May June July Aug. Sept. Oct. Nov. Dec.

Dorsal (above)
tailless
brown

Ventral (below)
white-rimmed black spots
prominent row of bright coral spots

Male

Female pg. 231   Larva

Comments: Living up to its name, male Purplish
Coppers have an iridescent purple sheen on the wings
above that is stunning when seen in sunlight. Primarily
relegated to moist areas, colonies tend to be small and
highly localized. Expanding agricultural activities, urban
development and habitat degradation have severely
restricted the butterfly's range and population in Ohio.
Now severely imperiled, it is one of seven butterflies
listed by the Ohio DNR as endangered. It is being bred
and reintroduced by the Toledo Zoological Gardens.
Males perch low on grasses or other vegetation with
their wings partially open to await passing females.

Purplish Copper
Lycaena helloides

Family/Subfamily: Gossamer Wings (Lycaenidae)/ Coppers (Lycaeninae)

Wingspan: 1.0–1.2" (2.5–3.0 cm)

Above: male is brown with a strong purplish iridescence and scattered black; female is primarily orange with scattered black spots and broad brown borders; hind-wing has a broad scalloped orange submarginal band

Below: forewing is orange with scattered black spots and a purplish brown apex and outer margin; hindwing purplish brown with small black spots and a narrow, irregular reddish orange submarginal line

Sexes: dissimilar; female has increased orange scaling on both wings

Egg: greenish white, laid singly on the host

Larva: green with several yellow stripes

Larval Host Plants: knotweed and dock

Habitat: open, moist habitats including wet meadows, stream margins, roadside ditches, pond margins, fallow agricultural land and marshes

Broods: two or more generations

Abundance: rare; localized

Compare: American (pg. 237) and Bronze (pg. 159) Coppers have silvery gray ventral hindwings. Bronze also has a wide reddish orange submarginal band.

Resident

Jan. Feb. Mar. Apr. May June July Aug. Sept. Oct. Nov. Dec.

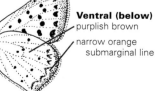

male

Dorsal (above)
iridescent purple/brown (both wings)

zig-zag orange outer margin

Ventral (below)
purplish brown

narrow orange submarginal line

Larvae

Comments: The Banded Hairstreak is Ohio's most abundant representative of this genus comprising primarily dull brown species. A small, inconspicuous butterfly of mixed hardwood forests with hickories and oaks, it may be readily encountered at flowers in nearby clearings or along adjacent roadsides. The adults are particularly fond of white sweet clover. Males perch on shrubs or low, overhanging limbs and aggressively dart out at other hairstreaks.

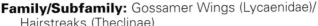

Banded Hairstreak
Satyrium calanus

Family/Subfamily: Gossamer Wings (Lycaenidae)/ Hairstreaks (Theclinae)

Wingspan: 1.00–1.25" (2.5–3.2 cm)

Above: unmarked dark brown with two hindwing tails

Below: variable; brown to slate gray; hindwing has dark postmedian band outlined on outer side with white and a red-capped black spot and blue patch near tails

Sexes: similar

Egg: pinkish brown, laid singly on twigs of host

Larva: variable, green to grayish brown with a light lateral stripe

Larval Host Plants: various oaks, hickories and walnuts including White Oak, Northern Red Oak, Pignut Hickory, Shagbark Hickory, Black Walnut and Bitternut

Habitat: mixed deciduous forests, oak woodlands, forest clearing, roadsides, old fields, parks, utility easements and suburban gardens

Broods: single generation

Abundance: occasional to common

Compare: Edwards' Hairstreak (pg. 109) has row of white-rimmed oval black spots, not dashes, below. Hickory Hairstreak (pg. 111) is extremely similar and may not reliably be separated in the field. Faded individuals may not be reliably identified.

Resident

Jan. Feb. Mar. Apr. May June July Aug. Sept. Oct. Nov. Dec.

Dorsal (above)
unmarked brown
two tails

Ventral (below)
band of darkened dashes edged outwardly in white
red-capped black spot
blue patch not capped in red

107

Larva

Comments: Edwards' Hairstreak is closely associated with dry areas dominated by short, scrubby oaks. Its relatively short flight period and resemblance to other, more abundant hairstreaks make it easy to overlook. Despite its overall rarity, it can be locally numerous. The developing, slug-like larvae are regularly tended (and guarded from predators) by Appalachian Mound Ants (*Fornica exoides*). In return for their protection, the ants receive food from the larvae in the form of nutritious sugar-rich secretions. It may rely heavily on the ants for survival, which may contribute to the butterfly's spotty and highly localized distribution.

Edwards' Hairstreak
Satyrium edwardsii

Family/Subfamily: Gossamer Wings (Lycaenidae)/
Hairstreaks (Theclinae)

Wingspan: 1.00–1.25" (2.5–3.2 cm)

Above: unmarked brown with a small orange spot near
short tail; male has small dark forewing stigma

Below: light gray brown with a row of small, white-
rimmed black spots; hindwing has a large blue patch
and a series of orange spots near tails

Sexes: similar, although female has slightly more
rounded wings and lacks dark forewing stigma above

Egg: cream pink, laid singly on host twigs near buds;
eggs overwinter

Larva: dark brown with dark dorsal band and a series of
pale oblique dashes along the sides

Larval Host Plants: various oaks including Scrub Oak,
Black Oak, Blackjack Oak and White Oak

Habitat: prairie hills, ridges, open oak barrens, forest
margins, roadsides, utility easements and trail margins

Broods: single generation

Abundance: rare to uncommon; localized

Compare: Striped (pg. 119) and Banded (pg. 107)
Hairstreaks have bands of white-edged dashes, not
distinctly separated white-rimmed dark oval spots, on
the wings below.

Resident

Jan. Feb. Mar. Apr. May June July Aug. Sept. Oct. Nov. Dec.

Dorsal (above)
unmarked brown

Ventral (below)
white-rimmed black
spots

orange spots

blue patch; often has
narrow orange cap

109

Comments: The Hickory Hairstreak is an uncommon butterfly of mixed deciduous forests and second growth woodlands. As its name implies, it utilizes a variety of hickories and walnuts as larval hosts. Populations tend to be small and highly localized in occurrence. In addition to its rarity, the species may further be overlooked because of its close resemblance to the more widespread and abundant Banded Hairstreak with which it often flies. The adults often perch high on the branches of their hosts and aggressively dart out at passing butterflies with a fast, erratic flight before alighting again.

Hickory Hairstreak
Satyrium caryaevorum

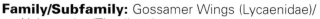

Family/Subfamily: Gossamer Wings (Lycaenidae)/ Hairstreaks (Theclinae)

Wingspan: 1.00–1.25" (2.5–3.2 cm)

Above: uniform dark brown with a short hindwing tail; male has a gray forewing stigma

Below: brown with a row of fairly wide and somewhat offset dark dashes edged in white across both wings, a large blue hindwing patch and orange-capped black spot near the tail

Sexes: similar, although female lacks forewing stigma

Egg: pinkish brown, laid singly on twigs; eggs overwinter

Larva: yellow green, often with dark green dorsal stripe, yellow lateral stripe and dark dashes edged in white

Larval Host Plants: various hickories, walnuts and oaks including Pignut Hickory, Shagbark Hickory, Bitternut Hickory, Northern Red Oak and Bitternut

Habitat: mixed deciduous forests, forest clearings, oak savannas, old fields and semi-open brushy areas

Broods: single generation

Abundance: rare to occasional

Compare: Edwards' Hairstreak (pg. 109) has row of white-rimmed oval black spots, not dashes, below. Banded Hairstreak (pg. 107) is extremely similar and may not reliably be separated in the field. Faded individuals may not be reliably identified. Resident

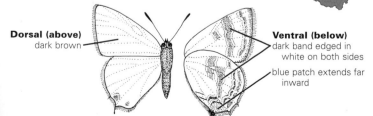

Jan. Feb. Mar. Apr. May June July Aug. Sept. Oct. Nov. Dec.

Dorsal (above)
dark brown

Ventral (below)
dark band edged in white on both sides

blue patch extends far inward

111

Male   Female   Larva

Comments: Although widespread throughout much of the East, this small species is seldom overly abundant in Ohio. Easily confused with the similar Tawny-edged Skipper, the two can often be distinguished on the basis of habitat, with the Crossline Skipper preferring much drier locations. Adults have a low, rapid flight and often alight on low vegetation. Males may occasionally be encountered sipping moisture at mud puddles.

Crossline Skipper
Polites origenes

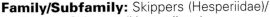

Family/Subfamily: Skippers (Hesperiidae)/ Banded Skippers (Hesperiinae)

Wingspan: 1.00–1.25" (2.5–3.2 cm)

Above: male is dark olive brown; forewing has tawny orange scaling along costal margin and yellow orange spots along the outer edge of black stigma

Below: hindwing is yellow brown with a faint, straight band of small pale spots; forewing has dull tawny orange scaling along costal margin, not strongly contrasting with color of hindwing

Sexes: dissimilar; female darker above with cream spots on forewing and reduced orange along costal margin

Egg: greenish, laid singly on host leaves

Larva: dark brown with faint white mottling and a round black head

Larval Host Plants: various grasses including Little Bluestem, Purpletop Grass, mannagrass and bluegrass

Habitat: dry, grassy areas including old fields, woodland meadows, pastures, prairies, forest clearings and utility easements

Broods: two generations

Abundance: uncommon to occasional

Compare: Tawny-edged Skipper (pg. 95) prefers wetter habitats, is smaller, and usually has unmarked, darker hindwings.

Resident

Jan. Feb. Mar. Apr. May June July Aug. Sept. Oct. Nov. Dec.

male

Dorsal (above)
orange scaling
yellow orange spots
long straight stigma
faint orange scaling

Ventral (below)
dull orange scaling
faint, straight band of small pale spots

113

Female

Larva

Comments: What this skipper lacks in size it more than
makes up for in sheer numbers, being one of Ohio's
most abundant species. Primarily a butterfly of moist
meadows and marshes, it tolerates a wide range of
more human-disturbed, grassy areas including roadsides and suburban lawns. The small adults maneuver
close to the ground with a rapid, darting flight but regularly alight on low vegetation. Its distinctive yellow
ventral hindwing patch is somewhat variable in appearance and may be continuous or broken into separate
spots.

Peck's Skipper
Polites peckius

Family/Subfamily: Skippers (Hesperiidae)/ Banded Skippers (Hesperiinae)

Wingspan: 1.00–1.25" (2.5–3.2 cm)

Above: dark brown; forewing has orange scaling toward base and a few tiny orange spots near apex; hindwing has a band of elongated narrow orange spots

Below: variable; hindwing is dark brown with a distinctive irregular central golden yellow patch

Sexes: similar, although female has reduced orange scaling at forewing base

Egg: whitish green, laid singly on host leaves

Larva: dark maroon brown with short light hairs and a black head and anal patch

Larval Host Plants: various grasses including Rice Cutgrass and Kentucky Bluegrass

Habitat: open grassy areas including pastures, roadsides, old fields, wet meadows, marshes, utility easements and lawns

Broods: two generations

Abundance: occasional to abundant

Compare: unique

Resident

Jan. Feb. Mar. Apr. May June July Aug. Sept. Oct. Nov. Dec.

Dorsal (above)
orange scaling
dark brown borders

Ventral (below)
variable central golden yellow patch; often fused or separated into component spots

115

Larva

Comments: Although previously treated as a separate species (the Northern Hairstreak), populations outside of the Florida peninsula and the extreme southern Atlantic Coast are now recognized to be geographic races of the same butterfly. The Southern Hairstreak inhabits oak-dominated woodlands and adjacent open areas. While it is generally uncommon in Ohio, this is one of the best places to find this hairstreak in the northeastern U.S. Colonies tend to be small and local. Adults have a quick, erratic flight and frequently perch high on the leaves of surrounding vegetation, regularly venturing down to nectar at a variety of small blossoms.

Southern Hairstreak
Fixsenia favonius ontario

Family/Subfamily: Gossamer Wings (Lycaenidae)/ Hairstreaks (Theclinae)

Wingspan: 1.0–1.3" (2.5–3.3 cm)

Above: dark brown with dark forewing stigma and a small orange spot near the tails

Below: gray-brown with a white postmedian line strongly zigzagged toward hindwing tails, a large blue patch often capped lightly in orange, and short row of small orange spots, the largest of which borders a black spot

Sexes: similar

Egg: pinkish brown, laid singly on twigs; eggs overwinter

Larva: pale green; covered with tiny yellow dots

Larval Host Plants: various oaks including Black Oak, White Oak and Red Oak

Habitat: woodlands with oaks, and adjacent margins, clearings, roadsides, fields and utility easements

Broods: single generation

Abundance: rare to occasional

Compare: White M Hairstreak (pg. 83) has single red ventral hindwing spot. Gray Hairstreak (pg. 215) is light gray below with a less jagged white line.

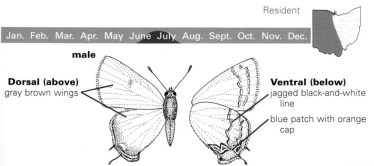

Resident

Jan. Feb. Mar. Apr. May June July Aug. Sept. Oct. Nov. Dec.

male

Dorsal (above)
gray brown wings

Ventral (below)
jagged black-and-white line

blue patch with orange cap

Larva

Comments: The Striped Hairstreak's name comes from the numerous white-edged dark dashes that give it an overall striped appearance. Although widespread throughout the state, it is generally uncommon, highly localized and seldom seen in any numbers. Adults are often encountered alongside a variety of other similar hairstreaks at available flowers. Females lay the small, flattened eggs singly on host twigs. The eggs overwinter and the young larvae hatch the following spring to feed on the buds and young leaves.

Striped Hairstreak
Satyrium liparops

Family/Subfamily: Gossamer Wings (Lycaenidae)/
Hairstreaks (Theclinae)

Wingspan: 1.0–1.3" (2.5–3.3 cm)

Above: unmarked dark brown with two hindwing tails

Below: brown to slate gray with numerous wide, dark
bands outlined in white; hindwing has an orange-
capped blue patch and several red spots near tails

Sexes: similar

Egg: pinkish brown, flattened, laid singly on twigs of host

Larva: bright green with yellow-green oblique stripes and
dark dorsal line

Larval Host Plants: various trees and shrubs in the
heath and rose families including flame azalea,
Highbush Blueberry, Sparkleberry, Black Cherry, Wild
Cherry, serviceberry and hawthorn

Habitat: mixed deciduous forests, thickets, forest clearings, woodland edges and adjacent open areas

Broods: single generation

Abundance: rare to occasional; localized

Compare: Banded (pg. 107) and Hickory (pg. 111)
Hairstreaks have less extensive, narrower ventral
bands and lack orange cap over blue hindwing patch.
Edwards' Hairstreak (pg. 109) has white-rimmed
dark oval spots, not dashes, on the
wings below.

Resident

Jan. Feb. Mar. Apr. May June July Aug. Sept. Oct. Nov. Dec.

Dorsal (above)
unmarked brown

Ventral (below)
wide, dark bands
outlined in white

blue patch with orange
cap

119

Dorsal

Larva

Comments: As its name implies, this small drab species is the most widespread and abundant roadside-skipper in Ohio. Nonetheless, it is seldom encountered in large numbers and often fairly local. Look for the butterfly in forest opening and other sun-dappled wooded sites. Like many small skippers, its flight is quick and low to the ground. Adults are often observed on low perches or nectaring at nearby blossoms, where they tend to be rather wary of close approach. Males often sip moisture at damp earth.

Common Roadside-Skipper
Amblyscirtes vialis

Family/Subfamily: Skippers (Hesperiidae)/ Banded Skippers (Hesperiinae)

Wingspan: 1.0–1.3" (2.5–3.3 cm)

Above: primarily dark blackish brown with a few small white spots near the forewing apex

Below: dark grayish black with faint gray frosting; forewing has a few small white spots (sometimes fused into a tapering band) near the apex

Sexes: similar

Egg: pale green, laid singly on host leaves

Larva: pale green with a whitish head marked with reddish brown vertical lines

Larval Host Plants: various grasses including Indian Woodoats, Bermuda Grass and bentgrass

Habitat: sunlit forest clearings, woodland margins, stream corridors, utility easements and adjacent fields

Broods: two generations

Abundance: occasional; localized

Compare: Pepper and Salt Skipper (pg. 101) has heavy gray overscaling and a cream postmedian spot band on the hindwing below.

Resident

Jan. Feb. Mar. Apr. May June July Aug. Sept. Oct. Nov. Dec.

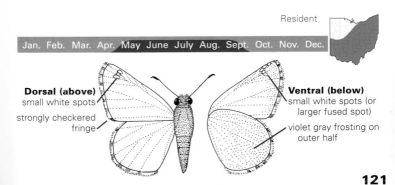

Dorsal (above)
small white spots

strongly checkered fringe

Ventral (below)
small white spots (or larger fused spot)

violet gray frosting on outer half

Male

Male | Female | Female variant | Larva

Comments: The Mulberry Wing occurs in a limited patchwork range from Massachusetts west to Minnesota. It is a small and extremely distinctive skipper of sedge-dominated wetlands. Restricted by its habitat, it typically occurs in small and very highly localized populations that may be overlooked. As a result, it is poorly known with little detailed information available on its biology and life history. Adults flutter low with a slow, feeble flight somewhat reminiscent of the Least Skipper's. They alight frequently and are most often observed at nearby flowers or when flushed into the air by disturbances in their habitat.

Mulberry Wing
Poanes massasoit

Family/Subfamily: Skippers (Hesperiidae)/
Banded Skippers (Hesperiinae)

Wingspan: 1.0–1.4" (2.5–3.6 cm)

Above: dark blackish brown with a few scattered yellow-orange spots; forewings are noticeably rounded

Below: forewing is unmarked dark blackish brown; hindwing is dark blackish brown with a golden yellow postmedian band intersected by a wide central ray

Sexes: similar, although female has slightly larger white dorsal spots

Egg: white, laid singly on host

Larva: currently undocumented

Larval Host Plants: various sedges including Upright Sedge

Habitat: swamps, marshes, wet grassy meadows, fens, roadside ditches, woodland margins and other open wetland sites

Abundance: rare to occasional; localized

Broods: single generation

Compare: unique

Resident

| Jan. | Feb. | Mar. | Apr. | May | June | July | Aug. | Sept. | Oct. | Nov. | Dec. |

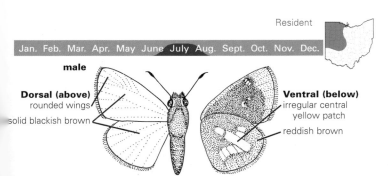

male

Dorsal (above)
rounded wings
solid blackish brown

Ventral (below)
irregular central
yellow patch

reddish brown

123

Female

Ventral

Larva

Comments: Hayhurst's Scallopwing is named for the distinctive scalloped hindwing margins that quickly distinguish it from all other small dark skippers in the state. Although often favoring shaded, moist woodland habitats, it can also be encountered in a variety of more open, disturbed sites in close association with its introduced weedy larval host. The butterfly likely utilizes several native members of the Amaranth family as well. Adults have a quick, scurrying flight and regularly perch or nectar with their wings outstretched, providing a prominent view of their namesake wing shape.

Hayhurst's Scallopwing
Staphylus hayhurstii

Family/Subfamily: Skippers (Hesperiidae)/ Spread-wing Skippers (Pyrginae)

Wingspan: 1.0–1.4" (2.5–3.6 cm)

Above: dark blackish brown with black bands and subtle gold flecking; forewing has a few small white spots; hindwing has distinctly scalloped margin

Below: forewing is marked as above but paler

Sexes: similar, although female is lighter brown with an overall more banded appearance

Egg: pink, laid singly on the underside of host leaves

Larva: green with a pinkish hue, a dark green dorsal stripe, a thin yellow lateral stripe, and a black head

Larval Host Plants: Lamb's Quarters

Habitat: shady wooded stream margins, weedy disturbed sites, fallow agricultural land, forest edges and gardens

Broods: two generations

Abundance: rare; localized

Compare: unique

Resident Visitor

Jan. Feb. Mar. Apr. May June July Aug. Sept. Oct. Nov. Dec.

female

Dorsal (above)

small glassy spots

subtle black bands

checkered fringe

scalloped margin

Ventral (below)

Female

Male pg. 243   Female   Male   Larva

Comments: The Zabulon Skipper is strikingly dimorphic with bright orange males and purplish brown females. A denizen of wooded habitats, the butterfly is most often encountered in dappled sunlit patches along forest trails or clearings. Nonetheless, individuals will wander into nearby, more open landscapes in search of available nectar resources. The pugnacious males perch on branches around head-height to await passing mates and aggressively fly out to engage rival males before returning to the same or nearby perch moments later. Females generally prefer to remain within the confines of shadier locales.

Zabulon Skipper
Poanes zabulon

Family/Subfamily: Skippers (Hesperiidae)/
Banded Skippers (Hesperiinae)

Wingspan: 1.0–1.4" (2.5–3.6 cm)

Above: male is golden orange with dark brown borders
and small brown spot near forewing apex; female is
dark brown with band of cream spots across forewing

Below: male hindwing yellow with a brown base enclosing a yellow spot; female is dark brown with small
light subapical spots, lavender scaling on wing margins, and white bar along leading margin of hindwing

Sexes: dissimilar, female brown with little orange color

Egg: pale green, laid singly on host leaves

Larva: tan with dark dorsal stripe, white lateral stripe and
short, light-colored hairs; reddish brown head

Larval Host Plants: various grasses including
Purpletop Grass, Whitegrass and lovegrass

Habitat: uncommon to occasional

Broods: two generations

Abundance: uncommon to occasional

Compare: Female "Pocahontas" form of Hobomok
Skipper (pg. 165) lacks white bar along the leading
margin of the ventral hindwing.

Resident

Jan. Feb. Mar. Apr. May June July Aug. Sept. Oct. Nov. Dec.

male

Dorsal (above)
dark spot
narrow black cell
end bar
golden orange
clear golden
orange

Ventral (below)
dark base encloses
yellow spot
yellow with darker
spots

127

Dorsal

Larva

Comments: This widespread eastern skipper was once
considered the same species as the Southern Broken-
Dash. The species' unique name comes from the dark
forewing stigma that is separated or "broken" into
two distinct dashes. Encountered in open habitats bordering woodlands, it readily ventures into nearby
gardens in search of nectar. Although ranging far to
the north, it is actually much more common in the
Southeast. Adults are highly active butterflies but frequently stop to perch or feed where they can be easily
and closely observed.

Northern Broken-Dash
Wallengrenia egeremet

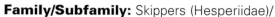

Family/Subfamily: Skippers (Hesperiidae)/ Banded Skippers (Hesperiinae)

Wingspan: 1.0–1.5" (2.5–3.8 cm)

Above: dark brown; forewing has yellow orange scaling along the costal margin, a distinct separated stigma and an elongated bright yellow orange spot extending outward from the tip of the stigma

Below: hindwing is yellow brown with central band of faint, light spots

Sexes: dissimilar; female is primarily dark brown above with a few elongated cream yellow forewing spots and reduced yellow orange markings

Egg: green, laid singly on host leaves

Larva: light green with darker green mottling, yellow lateral stripes; dark brown head with faint vertical stripes

Larval Host Plants: various grasses including Switchgrass and Deertongue

Habitat: open, sunny areas near woodlands including forest clearings and margins, roadsides, fallow agricultural land, pastures, old fields and gardens

Broods: single generation

Abundance: occasional to common

Compare: Little Glassywing (pg. 131) has prominent square glassy spots on the forewing above.

Resident

Jan. Feb. Mar. Apr. May June July Aug. Sept. Oct. Nov. Dec.

male

Dorsal (above)
yellow orange spot at end of stigma
"broken" black stigma

Ventral (below)
dull yellow brown
light spot band

129

Dorsal

Larva

Comments: The Little Glassywing is named for the distinct translucent or "glassy" white spots on its forewing. It is a butterfly of shaded forest margins and adjacent, moist habitats or even open fields but is not readily encountered in home gardens. Populations tend to be fairly small and somewhat local. Adults have a low, quick flight and readily visit available wildflowers. Males perch on low growing vegetation in sunny areas for females.

Little Glasswing
Pompeius verna

Family/Subfamily: Skippers (Hesperiidae)/
Banded Skippers (Hesperiinae)

Wingspan: 1.0–1.5" (2.5–3.8 cm)

Above: male is dark brown with black stigma and several semitransparent spots across forewing; female is dark brown with several semitransparent spots across forewing

Below: dark brown; hindwing purplish brown with band of faint, light spots

Sexes: similar; female darker with more rounded wings and larger forewing spots

Egg: white, laid singly on host leaves

Larva: green to greenish brown with dark mottling and stripes; head is reddish brown

Larval Host Plants: grasses including Purpletop Grass

Habitat: moist, open woodlands, forest edges, wetlands, roadsides, pastures, old fields and gardens

Broods: single generation

Abundance: occasional; localized

Compare: Dun Skipper (pg. 139) and Northern Broken-Dash (pg. 129) lack the prominent, somewhat square semitransparent spots on the forewing above. Dun also lacks the discrete central band on the ventral hindwing.

Resident

Jan. Feb. Mar. Apr. May June July Aug. Sept. Oct. Nov. Dec.

male

Dorsal (above)
semitransparent spots
(central spot
somewhat square)
black stigma

Ventral (below)
purplish brown
faint pale band

Female

Male pg. 245 | Female | Male | Larva

Comments: The Sachem has an affinity for just about any open, sunny habitat. This southern butterfly regularly wanders northward and may periodically colonize portions of Ohio. Temporary breeding populations are sporadic, but can at times reach high densities. Adults have a very rapid, darting flight that is usually low to the ground. Exceedingly fond of flowers, they often form a circus of activity with several individuals pausing briefly to perch or nectar before one flies up and disturbs the others.

Sachem
Atalopedes campestris

Family/Subfamily: Skippers (Hesperiidae)/ Banded Skippers (Hesperiinae)

Wingspan: 1.0–1.5" (2.5–3.8 cm)

Above: elongated wings; male is golden orange with brown borders and large, black stigma; female is dark brown with golden markings in wing centers; forewing has black median spot and several semitransparent spots

Below: variable; hindwing golden brown in male, brown in female with pale postmedian patch or band of spots

Sexes: dissimilar; female darker with semitransparent forewing spots and reduced orange markings

Egg: white, laid singly on host leaves

Larva: greenish brown with thin, dark dorsal stripe and black head

Larval Host Plants: various grasses including Bermuda Grass and crabgrass

Habitat: open, disturbed areas including old fields, pastures, roadsides, parks, lawns and gardens

Broods: one or more generations

Abundance: rare to occasional

Compare: Fiery Skipper (pg. 235) has small dark spots on the hindwing below.

Visitor

Jan.	Feb.	Mar.	Apr.	May	June	July	Aug.	Sept.	Oct.	Nov.	Dec.

male

Dorsal (above)
elongated forewing
large squarish stigma
golden orange

Ventral (below)
large pale patch or postmedian spot band

133

Larva

Comments: Bearing Carolina's name, this small brown butterfly is one of the most abundant satyrs in the Southeast. Nonetheless, the species' range extends northward to just enter the extreme southern portion of Ohio. It frequents shady woodland clearings and adjacent open, grassy areas but tends to be fairly local and sporadic in occurrence. Adults have a low, erratic flight and bob slowly along among understory vegetation or through tall grass. Between periodic bursts of activity, adults perch on grasses or leaf litter with their wings tightly closed and can be easily approached for observation.

Carolina Satyr
Hermeuptychia sosybius

Family/Subfamily: Brush-foots (Nymphalidae)/ Satyrs and Wood Nymphs (Satyrinae)

Wingspan: 1.0–1.5" (2.5–3.8 cm)

Above: dark brown with no distinct markings or eyespots

Below: brown with two narrow, dark brown lines through center of wings; hindwing has row of yellow-rimmed dark eyespots

Sexes: similar

Egg: green, laid singly on host leaves

Larva: pale green with darker green longitudinal stripes and short yellow hairs

Larval Host Plants: various grasses including Broadleaf Carpetgrass and Bermuda Grass

Habitat: woodlands, forest clearings, trails and roadsides and adjacent disturbed, grassy areas

Broods: two generations

Abundance: uncommon to locally common

Compare: Little Wood Satyr (pg. 185) is larger and has two prominent yellow-rimmed eyespots on both wings above and below. Gemmed Satyr (pg. 161) lacks eyespots on the wings below.

Resident

| Jan. | Feb. | Mar. | Apr. | May | June | July | Aug. | Sept. | Oct. | Nov. | Dec. |

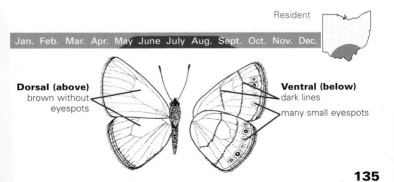

Dorsal (above)
brown without eyespots

Ventral (below)
dark lines

many small eyespots

135

Male

Larva

Comments: The Cobweb Skipper is named for the distinctively jagged pattern on the hindwing below that resembles a spider's web. On the wing for a single spring flight, look for it in clearings, disturbed areas or other grassy sites in close association with stands of its larval hosts. Colonies are typically of low density, spotty and highly localized, although it can be a fairly common butterfly when encountered. The adults have a rapid and extremely low flight. It is a wary butterfly but readily perches on or near the ground and visits a variety of low-growing spring flowers.

Cobweb Skipper
Hesperia metea

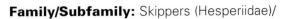

Family/Subfamily: Skippers (Hesperiidae)/
Banded Skippers (Hesperiinae)

Wingspan: 1.1–1.4" (2.8–3.6 cm)

Above: olive brown; forewing has tawny orange spots
and a narrow black stigma; hindwing has angled band
of tawny orange spots

Below: hindwing is olive brown with irregular white
bands and veins giving an overall cobweb appearance

Sexes: dissimilar; female is primarily dark brown with a
few pale forewing spots near the apex

Egg: white, laid singly on or near host leaves

Larva: gray brown with a dark dorsal stripe and a round
black head

Larval Host Plants: various grasses including Little
Bluestem and Big Bluestem

Habitat: woodland clearings, pastures, utility easements,
old fields and recently cleared or burned sites

Broods: single generation

Abundance: occasional; localized

Compare: unique

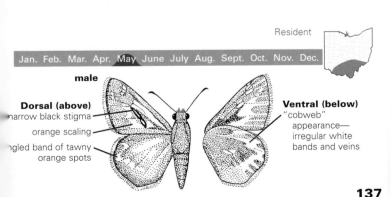

Resident

Jan. Feb. Mar. Apr. May June July Aug. Sept. Oct. Nov. Dec.

male

Dorsal (above)
narrow black stigma
orange scaling
angled band of tawny
orange spots

Ventral (below)
"cobweb"
appearance—
irregular white
bands and veins

Male

Larva

Comments: The Dun Skipper is a small, chocolate brown butterfly with few markings. Although preferring moist, grassy or sedge-dominated areas associated with deciduous woodlands, it frequently ventures into surrounding open habitats and is periodically encountered in home gardens. Adults have a quick, low flight and dart around erratically over the vegetation. It is an avid flower visitor readily drawn to available blossoms. Males occasionally visit damp ground.

Dun Skipper
Euphyes vestris

Family/Subfamily: Skippers (Hesperiidae)/
Banded Skippers (Hesperiinae)

Wingspan: 1.0–1.5" (2.5–3.8 cm)

Above: male is dark chocolate brown with black stigma;
female is dark brown with several whitish spots on
forewing

Below: brown; typically unmarked hindwing, but occasionally has faint spot band

Sexes: similar; female has small, white forewing spots

Egg: green, laid singly on host leaves

Larva: green with thin white lines; head is brown with
light outer stripes and dark center

Larval Host Plants: various sedges including Upright
Sedge

Habitat: moist areas in or near deciduous woodlands,
wet meadows, marshes, forest margins, stream corridors, roadsides, pastures, prairies, fens, utility
easements and old fields

Broods: two generations

Abundance: occasional to common

Compare: Little Glassywing (pg. 131) has distinct glassy
white spots on forewing and defined ventral hindwing
band.

Resident

| Jan. | Feb. | Mar. | Apr. | May | June | July | Aug. | Sept. | Oct. | Nov. | Dec. |

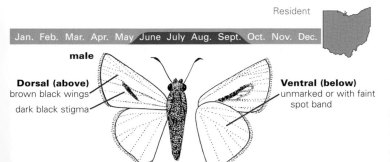

male

Dorsal (above)
brown black wings

dark black stigma

Ventral (below)
unmarked or with faint
spot band

Comments: This lovely gray hairstreak is restricted to wetland habitats or other moist areas that support willows. Although widespread across much of the Northeast and Great Lakes, the species tends to occur in relatively small, highly localized colonies but can be rather common when encountered. Adults have a quick, erratic flight and are most often observed at nearby moisture-loving flowers. They are particularly fond of milkweed blossoms.

Acadian Hairstreak
Satyrium acadica

Family/Subfamily: Gossamer Wings (Lycaenidae)/ Hairstreaks (Theclinae)

Wingspan: 1.10–1.45" (2.8–4.0 cm)

Above: brown with a small orange crescent-shaped hind-wing spot above a short tail

Below: uniform gray with a postmedian row of round, white-rimmed black spots; hindwing has a submarginal row of orange crescent-shaped spots and a orange-capped blue patch near the tail

Sexes: similar

Egg: white, laid singly on host twigs; eggs overwinter

Larva: green and white lateral stripe, pale white oblique dashes, and a darker green dorsal stripe edged in white

Larval Host Plants: various willows

Habitat: stream margins, pond edges, marshes, swamps, wet roadside ditches, depressions, bogs and moist meadows

Broods: single generation

Abundance: uncommon to occasional; localized

Compare: Edwards' Hairstreak (pg. 109) has gray-brown ventral wings and is typically found in more xeric (dry) habitats with oaks

Resident

| Jan. | Feb. | Mar. | Apr. | May | June | July | Aug. | Sept. | Oct. | Nov. | Dec. |

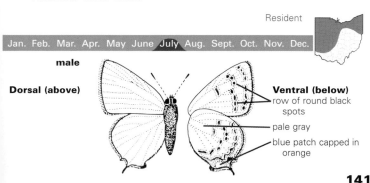

male

Dorsal (above)

Ventral (below)
row of round black spots

pale gray

blue patch capped in orange

Male

Larva

Comments: The Dreamy Duskywing is a small, early spring species common throughout much of boreal North America. Within Ohio, it is most frequently encountered in the northern portions of the state. Both it and the similar but somewhat larger Sleepy Duskywing lack the glassy forewing spots that characterize all other members of this group. Adults scurry low to the ground along forest trails or margins with a fast, bouncing flight. Males perch low on the ends of bare twigs or in sunlit patches of soil to await passing females and are often encountered puddling at moist areas.

Dreamy Duskywing
Erynnis icelus

Family/Subfamily: Skippers (Hesperiidae)/
Spread-wing Skippers (Pyrginae)

Wingspan: 1.0–1.6" (2.5–4.1 cm)

Above: dark brown; forewing has extensive gray scaling
toward outer margin, two black chain-like bands
enclosing a broad gray patch, a dark base, lacks glassy
spots; hindwing has two rows of pale spots; labial
palpi are noticeably long and project forward

Below: dark brown, hindwing has two rows of pale spots

Sexes: similar, although female is lighter with more heavily patterned forewings

Egg: green turning reddish, laid singly on stems or leaves

Larva: pale green with a dark dorsal stripe, a white lateral stripe, numerous tiny white tubercles, and a black
head marked with yellow and red spots

Larval Host Plants: various willows, poplars and
birches

Habitat: open woodlands, forest edges and clearings,
roadsides, moist woodland depressions

Broods: single generation

Abundance: rare to common

Compare: Sleepy Duskywing (pg. 170) flies earlier and is
larger with shorter, more rounded forewings.

Resident

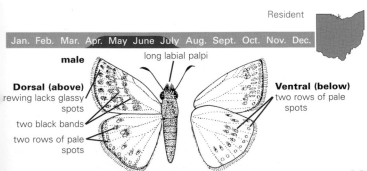

| Jan. | Feb. | Mar. | Apr. | May | June | July | Aug. | Sept. | Oct. | Nov. | Dec. |

male

long labial palpi

Dorsal (above)
rewing lacks glassy
spots

two black bands

two rows of pale
spots

Ventral (below)
two rows of pale
spots

143

Male

Ventral

Larva

Comments: The Two-spotted Skipper is a reclusive
species of sedge-dominated wetlands. Considered a
rare butterfly throughout Ohio, populations tend to be
small and highly localized in occurrence. Like many
other habitat-restricted species, it has declined as a
result of ever-expanding human activity and urban
development. Despite its distinctive ventral markings,
the species is named for two small white spots on the
upper surface of the forewing in females. Males perch
low of grasses or sedges and readily fly out to engage
rival males before returning to the same vicinity
moments later.

Two-spotted Skipper
Euphyes bimacula

Family/Subfamily: Skippers (Hesperiidae)/ Banded Skippers (Hesperiinae)

Wingspan: 1.25–1.40" (3.2–3.6 cm)

Above: dark brown with white fringes; forewing has small tawny orange patch and black stigma

Below: brownish orange with pale veins and a whitish anal hindwing margin

Sexes: dissimilar; female is primarily dark brown with two cream spots in the center of the forewing above

Egg: green, laid singly on host leaves

Larva: pale green with a darker dorsal stripe and numerous tiny wavy white dashes; reddish brown head marked with a black oval ringed in cream on the forehead, and a cream band around the outer margin

Larval Host Plants: various sedges including Upright Sedge

Habitat: wet meadows, fens and occasionally moist roadsides

Broods: single generation

Abundance: rare; localized

Compare: Crossline Skipper (pg. 113) lacks the white anal margin and pale veins on the ventral hindwing. Ventral hindwing typically also has faint postmedian band.

Resident

| Jan. | Feb. | Mar. | Apr. | May | June | July | Aug. | Sept. | Oct. | Nov. | Dec. |

male

Dorsal (above)
tawny orange scaling
white fringe

Ventral (below)
paler veins
white anal margin

Ventral

Larva

Comments: Aptly named, the Confused Cloudywing is often very tricky to distinguish from the more abundant Southern and Northern Cloudywings with which it often flies. Causing much of the problem is its band of glassy forewing spots that varies from highly reduced to prominent. A resident of the Southeast, it wanders north each year to temporarily colonize many areas and is likely a rare vagrant to Ohio. It may occur more frequently, but goes unnoticed due to is similarity to the two other members of the genus. Poorly known and understood, little detailed information is available on the life history and behavior of this obscure butterfly.

Confused Cloudywing
Thorybes confusis

Family/Subfamily: Skippers (Hesperiidae)/
Spread-wing Skippers (Pyrginae)

Wingspan: 1.2–1.6" (3.0–4.1 cm)

Above: brown with a variable band of several glassy
white spots across the forewing and a light, checkered
fringe; hindwing is tapered slightly toward bottom;
antennal clubs are all brown

Below: forewing is marked as above but paler and with
gray frosting along outer margin; hindwing has two
faint dark brown bands across center and faint light
frosting along outer margin; pale face

Sexes: similar

Egg: pale green, laid singly on host leaves

Larva: greenish brown with a dark dorsal stripe and pale
lateral stripes; blackish head

Larval Host Plants: various legumes such as beggarweeds and bush clover

Habitat: open sites in or near woodlands including clearings, trails, old fields, pastures and forest margins

Broods: two generations

Abundance: rare

Compare: Northern Cloudywing (pg. 157) has a dark
face. Southern Cloudywing (pg. 149) has a prominent,
straight forewing spot band and a white spot on the
antennal club.

Stray

Jan. Feb. Mar. Apr. May June July Aug. Sept. Oct. Nov. Dec.

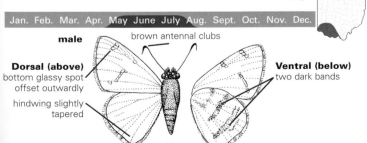

male

brown antennal clubs

Dorsal (above)
bottom glassy spot
offset outwardly

hindwing slightly
tapered

Ventral (below)
two dark bands

147

Ventral

Comments: Although called the Southern Cloudywing, the range of this dull brown skipper extends from Florida to the Canadian border. It is often found alongside the very similar Northern Cloudywing with which it is easily confused. Worn individuals can present a challenge even for experienced butterfly watchers. Adults have a strong, erratic flight but frequently stop to nectar. Males perch on low vegetation and aggressively dart out to investigate intruders before returning to the same general location moments later. Adults rest with their wings partially open but are often rather nervous and difficult to closely approach.

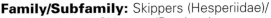

Southern Cloudywing
Thorybes bathyllus

Family/Subfamily: Skippers (Hesperiidae)/
Spread-wing Skippers (Pyrginae)

Wingspan: 1.2–1.6" (3.0–4.1 cm)

Above: brown with straight, glassy white spots across
forewing and light, checkered wing fringe; hindwing
tapered slightly toward bottom; antennal club has a
white spot

Below: brown; hindwing darker at base with two dark
brown bands; light face

Sexes: similar

Egg: green, laid singly on the leaves of host

Larva: greenish brown with black head, thin, dark dorsal
stripe and narrow light lateral stripe; body covered
with numerous short, light-colored hairs

Larval Host Plants: various legumes including beggarweeds, bush clover, Hog Peanut and milkvetch

Habitat: brushy fields, utility easements, forest edges,
dry woodlands and adjacent dry, open areas

Broods: single generation

Abundance: occasional to common

Compare: Northern Cloudywing (pg. 157) and Confused
Cloudywing (pg. 147) have smaller white dorsal
forewing spots.

Resident

| Jan. | Feb. | Mar. | Apr. | May | June | July | Aug. | Sept. | Oct. | Nov. | Dec. |

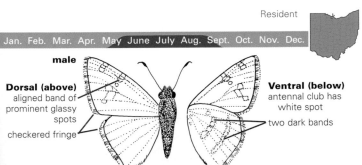

male

Dorsal (above)
aligned band of
prominent glassy
spots
checkered fringe

Ventral (below)
antennal club has
white spot
two dark bands

149

Ventral

Larva

Comments: This small and uncommon northern dusky-wing historically just entered the northwest corner of Ohio in the Oak Openings Region. Throughout its range, the Columbine Duskywing is primarily a butter-fly of wooded ravines, moist woodlands, and margins in very close association with patches of its larval host. It is easily confused with other duskywings and may not reliably be separated in the field except by habitat preference and host association. Adults have a quick, somewhat bouncing flight and maneuver erratically low among the vegetation. Both sexes readily nectar at a variety of available wildflowers.

Columbine Duskywing
Erynnis lucilius

Family/Subfamily: Skippers (Hesperiidae)/
Spread-wing Skippers (Pyrginae)

Wingspan: 1.2–1.6" (3.0–4.1 cm)

Above: dark brown with gray scaling; forewing is notice-ably darker basally with several small glassy spots toward the apex and an indistinct brown patch at the end of the cell

Below: dark brown; hindwing has marginal and submar-ginal rows of prominent light spots

Sexes: similar, although female is lighter with more heav-ily patterned wings and larger glassy spots

Egg: green, laid singly on host leaves

Larva: pale green with numerous tiny white tubercles, a dark green dorsal stripe and a white lateral stripe; dark brown head. Larvae construct individual shelters on the host by weaving two or more leaves together with silk. Larvae overwinter in individual leaf shelters and complete development the following spring.

Larval Host Plants: Wild Columbine

Habitat: moist woodlands and adjacent margins

Broods: two generations

Abundance: extirpated

Compare: Wild Indigo Duskywing (pg. 169) is slightly larger. May not be reliably distinguished in the field.

No longer present

Jan. Feb. Mar. Apr. May June July Aug. Sept. Oct. Nov. Dec.

Dorsal (above)
brown patch at
end of cell
indistinct

Ventral (below)
marginal and
submarginal rows
of distinct pale
spots

Larva

Comments: Finally an easy-to-identify duskywing! This small skipper can reliably be told apart from all other members of this complicated genus by its distinctively mottled wings. It is a rare to uncommon butterfly throughout its range and is typically found in isolated, sporadic colony sites. This species may need protection in Ohio, as no individuals have been witnessed for 15 years. The Mottled Duskywing can be encountered in open woodlands or in nearby brushy fields or prairies, often where the terrain is somewhat undulating. Males often puddle at damp ground with other duskywings but are rarely the most prevalent species present.

Mottled Duskywing
Erynnis martialis

Family/Subfamily: Skippers (Hesperiidae)/ Spread-wing Skippers (Pyrginae)

Wingspan: 1.2–1.6" (3.0–4.1 cm)

Above: brown and strongly patterned with numerous dark blotches giving a distinctive mottled appearance; forewing has several small glassy spots toward the apex; fresh individuals have a subtle violet sheen

Below: brown with numerous light and dark spots

Sexes: similar, although female is lighter with increased gray scaling and more heavily patterned wings

Egg: green soon turning pinkish, laid singly on host leaves

Larva: pale green with numerous tiny white tubercles and a black head marked with orange spots around the margin

Larval Host Plants: New Jersey Tea

Habitat: open upland woodland, forest edges and clearings, barrens and old fields

Broods: two generations

Abundance: rare; localized

Compare: unique

Resident

Jan. Feb. Mar. Apr. May June July Aug. Sept. Oct. Nov. Dec.

Dorsal (above)
glassy spots

both wings with strong mottling

sometimes has a faint violet sheen

Ventral (below)

153

Male

Larva

Comments: Generally an uncommon butterfly throughout its limited Midwestern range, the Black Dash is
restricted to marshes, wet meadows and other open
wetlands with abundant sedge. As a result, populations tend to be small and highly localized to suitable
habitat areas. The adults are swift on the wing but are
easily observed when feeding at nearby wetland wildflowers. Males perch like sentinels on tall grasses
watching keenly for passing females and readily fly out
to engage intruders.

Black Dash
Euphyes conspicua

Family/Subfamily: Skippers (Hesperiidae)/
Banded Skippers (Hesperiinae)

Wingspan: 1.25–1.60" (3.2–4.1 cm)

Above: golden-orange with broad, dark brown borders;
male has a broad black stigma

Below: hindwing orange-brown with a broad yellow postmedian patch

Sexes: dissimilar; female is primarily dark brown with
pale yellow forewing spots

Egg: laid singly on host

Larva: green with fine white mottling; brown head
marked with cream lines around the margin and a
black oval on the forehead

Larval Host Plants: various sedges including Upright
Sedge

Habitat: marshes, wet grassy meadows, fens, roadside
ditches, bogs, woodland margins and other open wetland sites

Abundance: uncommon to occasional; localized

Broods: single generation

Compare: Peck's Skipper (pg. 115) is smaller and
has yellow basal spots on the hindwing below.
Dion Skipper (pg. 257) is larger and has a long pale
ray through the hindwing without adjacent
postmedian spots.

Resident

Jan.	Feb.	Mar.	Apr.	May	June	July	Aug.	Sept.	Oct.	Nov.	Dec.

male

Dorsal (above)
heavy stigma
dark brown
borders
orange

Ventral (below)
red-brown hindwing
curved yellow patch

155

Ventral

Larva

Comments: The Northern Cloudywing is one of several similar-looking dark brown skippers found in Ohio. It is most likely to be confused with its close relative the Southern Cloudywing. The two species are often found together and require close examination to reliably separate. The adults have a low, skipping flight and quickly scurry along trails or clearings, occasionally pausing at a nearby flower to feed. Males perch on the ground or low on vegetation and aggressively dart out to engage rival males or passing females. At rest, they hold their wings in a relaxed, partially open position.

Northern Cloudywing
Thorybes pylades

Family/Subfamily: Skippers (Hesperiidae)/
Spread-wing Skippers (Pyrginae)

Wingspan: 1.2–1.7" (3.0–4.3 cm)

Above: brown with several small, elongated, misaligned glassy white spots on forewing and light, checkered wing fringe

Below: brown; hindwing darker at base with two dark brown bands; forewing has lavender gray scaling toward apex; dark face

Sexes: similar

Egg: pale greenish white, laid singly on the leaves of host

Larva: greenish brown with black head, thin, dark dorsal stripe and narrow pinkish brown lateral stripe; body covered with numerous short, light-colored hairs

Larval Host Plants: various legumes including beggar-weeds, bush clovers, milk vetch, Alfalfa and clovers

Habitat: open woodlands, forest edges, roadsides, utility easements, brushy fields and other dry, open areas

Broods: single generation

Abundance: occasional to common

Compare: Southern Cloudywing (pg. 149) has larger dorsal forewing spots that form an aligned band.

Resident

| Jan. | Feb. | Mar. | Apr. | May | June | July | Aug. | Sept. | Oct. | Nov. | Dec. |

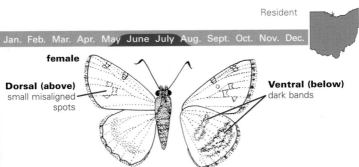

female

Dorsal (above)
small misaligned spots

Ventral (below)
dark bands

157

Male

Female pg. 253   Ventral   Larva

Comments: This sexually dimorphic species is our largest copper. Although primarily restricted to moist areas where its weedy larval hosts occur, it frequently wanders into nearby drier habitats in search of nectar. The Bronze Copper tends to occur in small, highly localized colonies but can be rather numerous when encountered. Like many other wetland species, it has suffered from the loss or degradation of available habitat. Males perch low on grasses or other vegetation with their wings partially open to await passing females.

Bronze Copper
Lycaena hyllus

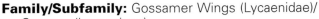

Family/Subfamily: Gossamer Wings (Lycaenidae)/ Coppers (Lycaeninae)

Wingspan: 1.25–1.65" (3.2–4.2 cm)

Above: male is brown with a purplish iridescence and a broad orange submarginal band containing black spots on the hindwing; female has light orange forewings with scattered black spots and a broad brown border; hindwing is purplish brown with a broad orange submarginal band containing black spots

Below: scattered white-rimmed black spots on both wings; forewing is orange with silvery gray apex and margin; hindwing is silvery gray with broad orange submarginal band containing black spots

Sexes: dissimilar; female is larger with rounder wings and increased orange scaling on the dorsal forewing

Egg: whitish, laid singly on host leaves or stems

Larva: yellow-green with a darker green dorsal stripe

Larval Host Plants: knotweed, Curly Dock, Water Dock

Habitat: open, moist habitats including fens, wet meadows and marshes; also adjacent clover fields

Broods: two or more generations

Abundance: uncommon to locally common

Compare: American (pg. 237) and Purplish (pg. 105) Coppers are smaller and have a narrow, reddish orange submarginal line on ventral hindwing.   Resident

Jan. Feb. Mar. Apr. May June July Aug. Sept. Oct. Nov. Dec.

male

Dorsal (above)
iridescent purple/brown above
orange band

Ventral (below)
pale orange forewing
small spots
silvery white hindwing
wide orange submarginal band

Larva

Comments: The Gemmed Satyr is one of our most
attractive satyrs and the only one without eyespots. At
home in moist, open woodlands, it may occasionally
wander into nearby drier habitats. The diminutive
adults dance along the forest floor with a weak, low
flight and can be a challenge to follow. They frequently
alight on leaf litter or among grassy vegetation.
Seldom very abundant, it occurs in spotty, highly localized colonies and may often be overlooked due to its
close resemblance to the Carolina Satyr.

Gemmed Satyr
Cyllopsis gemma

Family/Subfamily: Brush-foots (Nymphalidae)/
Satyrs and Wood Nymphs (Satyrinae)

Wingspan: 1.25–1.70" (3.2–4.3 cm)

Above: warm brown with very small dark spots along
hindwing margin

Below: light speckled brown with two narrow, dark wavy
lines through the center of the wings; hindwing has a
large purplish patch containing black spots with silver
highlights

Sexes: similar

Egg: green, laid singly on host leaves

Larva: green or brown with thin pale stripes, two small
tails and two brownish pink horns on the head

Larval Host Plants: Bermuda Grass

Habitat: open woodlands, stream corridors and associated shady grassy areas

Broods: three generations

Abundance: occasional to locally common

Compare: Carolina Satyr (pg. 135) has a row of yellow-
rimmed ventral eyespots on both the forewing and
hindwing.

Resident

Jan. Feb. Mar. Apr. May June July Aug. Sept. Oct. Nov. Dec.

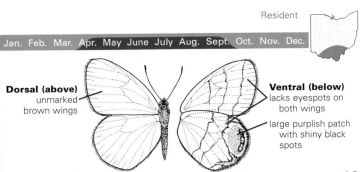

Dorsal (above)
unmarked
brown wings

Ventral (below)
lacks eyespots on
both wings

large purplish patch
with shiny black
spots

161

Female

Ventral

Larva

Comments: This rare duskywing occurs in scattered and often highly localized populations throughout the Midwest and Northeast. A butterfly of oak savannas and barrens, it is listed by the state as endangered. It shares its affinity for this specialized habitat with a few other imperiled butterflies including the Karner Blue and Frosted Elfin. Adults have a quick, somewhat bouncing flight and maneuver erratically low among the vegetation. Like other members of the genus, they roost at night on bare twigs with wings folded down around the branch. Larvae construct individual shelters by weaving two or more host leaves together with silk.

Persius Duskywing
Erynnis persius

Family/Subfamily: Skippers (Hesperiidae)/
Spread-wing Skippers (Pyrginae)

Wingspan: 1.25–1.70" (3.2–4.3 cm)

Above: dark brown with noticeable hair-like gray scaling; forewing is noticeably darker basally with several small glassy spots toward the apex and a distinctive gray patch at the end of the cell

Below: dark brown, hindwing has two rows of prominent light spots

Sexes: similar, although female is lighter with more heavily pattered wings and larger glassy spots

Egg: yellow-green, laid singly on the underside of host leaves

Larva: pale green with numerous tiny white tubercles, dark dorsal stripe and white lateral stripe; dark brown head marked with pale orange or yellow spots around the margin. Larvae overwinter in individual leaf shelters.

Larval Host Plants: a wide variety of plants in the bean family including Wild Indigo and Wild Lupine

Habitat: oak savannas and adjacent utility easements

Broods: single generation

Abundance: rare; localized

Compare: Wild Indigo Duskywing (pg. 169) lacks the prominent gray hair-like forewing scales. Flies from spring to fall.

Resident

Jan. Feb. Mar. Apr. May June July Aug. Sept. Oct. Nov. Dec.

male

Dorsal (above)
grayish patch at end of cell

numerous raised white hairs on upperside

Ventral (below)

163

Female "Pocahontas"

Male pg. 255 | Female | Ventral | Larva

Comments: This small woodland skipper has a single spring flight. Males perch on sunlit leaves and aggressively dart out at other passing butterflies. They may also frequently be encountered at wet earth along forested roads or trails. Although preferring shadier conditions, both sexes will venture into nearby open areas to nectar at early-season blossoms. Female Hobomoks produce two distinct forms. The lighter form resembles the male and the darker form "Pocahontas" is superficially similar to Zabulon Skipper females. Larvae construct individual leaf shelters on the host. Larvae overwinter.

Hobomok Skipper
Poanes hobomok

Family/Subfamily: Skippers (Hesperiidae)/
Banded Skippers (Hesperiinae)

Wingspan: 1.4–1.6" (3.6–4.1 cm)

Above: golden orange with irregular dark brown borders
and a narrow black cell-end bar on the forewing

Below: purplish brown with a broad yellow orange patch
through the hindwing

Sexes: dissimilar; female has two forms. Normal form
resembles male but has reduced orange scaling above.
"Pocahontas" form is dark brown above with pale
forewing spots; hindwing is purplish brown below with
faint band and violet gray frosting along outer margin.

Egg: white, laid singly on host leaves

Larva: brown green with numerous short, light-colored
hairs; round, brown head

Larval Host Plants: various grasses including Little
Bluestem, panic grasses, Poverty Oatgrass, bluegrass
and Rice Cutgrass

Habitat: open woodlands, forest edges, clearings and
trails, roadsides and along forested stream margins

Broods: single generation

Abundance: occasional to common

Compare: Female Zabulon Skipper (pg. 127) has a white
bar along leading edge of ventral hindwing.

Resident

| Jan. | Feb. | Mar. | Apr. | May | June | July | Aug. | Sept. | Oct. | Nov. | Dec. |

male

Dorsal (above)
narrow cell-end bar
no stigma
irregular dark brown
borders

Ventral (below)
purplish brown
broad yellow orange
patch

Male

Female   Female   Larva

Comments: This widespread eastern skipper frequently
wanders from its woodland habitat into nearby disturbed sites in search of nectar and may occasionally
show up in home gardens. Adults flutter about with
quick, somewhat erratic flight usually low to the ground.
Like other duskywings, they hold their wings outstretched when feeding or basking. Males perch on low
vegetation in sunlit spots to await passing females and
occasionally puddle at damp sand or gravel. The larvae
construct individual shelters on the host by folding over
leaves with silk. Once fully mature, larvae from the late
season generation overwinter among the leaf litter.

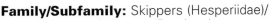

Horace's Duskywing
Erynnis horatius

Family/Subfamily: Skippers (Hesperiidae)/
Spread-wing Skippers (Pyrginae)

Wingspan: 1.25–1.75" (3.2–4.4 cm)

Above: dark brown overall with gray scaling usually lacking; forewing has cluster of small clear spots near apex and one at end of forewing cell; female is lighter with more contrasting pattern

Below: brown with faint rows of light spots along outer edge of hindwing

Sexes: similar, although female is lighter with more heavily patterned forewings and larger forewing spots

Egg: pale yellow green, laid singly on new growth of host

Larva: pale green with tiny white spots; reddish brown head marked with orange spots around the margin

Larval Host Plants: various oaks including Scrub Oak, Northern Red Oak and Post Oak

Habitat: oak woodlands, forest edges and clearings, roadsides, utility easements and nearby open areas

Broods: two generations

Abundance: uncommon to occasional

Compare: Juvenal's Duskywing (pg. 183) has two light spots along leading margin of ventral hindwing and extensive gray scaling on dorsal forewing.

Resident

Jan. Feb. Mar. Apr. May June July Aug. Sept. Oct. Nov. Dec.

male

Dorsal (above)
glassy spots

glassy spot at end
of cell

cks extensive gray
scaling

Ventral (below)
lacks spots along
leading margin

167

Male

Female

Larva

Comments: The Wild Indigo Duskywing is named for one of its preferred larval hosts. Generally common in open woodlands, prairies and scrubby fields, it has become more widespread because of its ability utilize the introduced groundcover Crown Vetch as a host. As a result, it is now often found along highways or other rights-of-way. It is often extremely abundant in late summer and early fall. The butterfly has a fast, erratic flight but readily stops to nectar or perch on sunlit leaves or twigs. Males frequently puddle at damp ground.

Wild Indigo Duskywing
Erynnis baptisiae

Family/Subfamily: Skippers (Hesperiidae)/
Spread-wing Skippers (Pyrginae)

Wingspan: 1.3–1.7 (3.3–4.3 cm)

Above: dark brown with pale spots; forewing has darker
base with several small glassy spots toward the apex
and a distinctive reddish brown patch at the end of the
cell; hindwing typically has faint cell-end bar

Below: dark brown, hindwing has two rows of prominent
light spots

Sexes: similar, although female is lighter with more heavily pattered wings and larger glassy spots

Egg: green, laid singly on host leaves

Larva: pale green with numerous tiny white tubercles,
dark dorsal stripe, white lateral stripe; dark brown head
marked with pale orange or yellow around the margin

Larval Host Plants: a wide variety of plants in the bean
family including Wild Indigo, Blue Wild Indigo, White
Wild Indigo, Canadian Milkvetch, Wild Lupine and
Crown Vetch

Habitat: open woodlands, prairies, forest edges and
clearings, roadsides, utility easements and old fields

Broods: two or three generations

Abundance: occasional to common

Compare: Horace's Duskywing (pg. 167) has glassy spot
at end of forewing cell.

Resident

| Jan. | Feb. | Mar. | Apr. | May | June | July | Aug. | Sept. | Oct. | Nov. | Dec. |

male

Dorsal (above)
red-brown spot at
end of cell

typically lacks glassy
spot at end of cell

basal half of wing
darker

faint cell-end bar

Ventral (below)
two rows of white
spots

169

Male

Female Ventral Larva

Comments: This early spring species is typically out before the smaller and similar-looking Dreamy Duskywing. Together, they are the only two dusky-wings in the state that lack small glassy forewing spots. They are often easy to confuse in the field. It is a widespread and generally common butterfly through-out much of the eastern U.S., but occasionally undergoes marked fluctuations in abundance. Adults perch and rest with their mottled gray-brown wings held in an open posture, a common characteristic of all duskywings. Larvae construct individual leaf shelters and overwinter inside, pupating the following spring.

Sleepy Duskywing
Erynnis brizo

Family/Subfamily: Skippers (Hesperiidae)/
Spread-wing Skippers (Pyrginae)

Wingspan: 1.30–1.75" (3.3–4.4 cm)

Above: dark brown; forewing has extensive gray scaling toward outer margin and two black chain-like bands; hindwing has two rows of faint pale spots

Below: dark brown, hindwing has two often faint rows of pale spots

Sexes: similar, female is lighter with more heavily patterned forewing and more prominent hindwing spots

Egg: green, laid singly on host leaves

Larva: pale green with a yellow white lateral stripe and numerous tiny white tubercles; brown head marked with six orange spots around the margin

Larval Host Plants: various oaks including Scrub Oak and Black Oak, also American Chestnut

Habitat: open oak woodlands and scrub, forest edges and clearings, roadsides and adjacent open sites

Broods: single generation

Abundance: uncommon to common

Compare: Dreamy Duskywing (pg. 143) is smaller, forewing has darker base and more distinct gray patch between black bands; flies later.

Resident

Jan. Feb. Mar. Apr. May June July Aug. Sept. Oct. Nov. Dec.

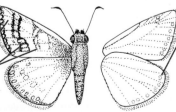

Dorsal (above)
cks glassy forewing spots

inct black, chainlike bands

Ventral (below)
faint spots

Comments: This lovely species once occurred from New Jersey to Michigan, including portions of northeastern Ohio. A butterfly of specialized wetlands called fens, Mitchell's Satyr has unfortunately disappeared from many of its former haunts as a result of habitat loss or alteration. Today, it is only reported in southern Michigan and extreme northern Indiana. It remains critically imperiled and is listed as both a state and federal endangered species. The adults have a slow, bobbing flight and maneuver low among the wetland vegetation stopping frequently to perch. Individual colonies tend to be small and are easily overlooked.

Mitchell's Satyr
Neonympha mitchellii

Family/Subfamily: Brush-foots (Nymphalidae)/
Satyrs and Wood Nymphs (Satyrinae)

Wingspan: 1.3–1.8" (3.3–4.6 cm)

Above: uniform unmarked brown

Below: brown with a submarginal row of rounded yellow-rimmed black eyespots bearing silvery blue highlights; two orange-brown lines across both wings

Sexes: similar, although female is slightly larger

Egg: cream, laid singly on host

Larva: elongate, green with longitudinal white stripes

Larval Host Plants: currently undocumented in the wild, but likely various sedges

Habitat: prairie fens

Broods: single generation

Abundance: rare; extirpated

Compare: unique

No longer present

Jan. Feb. Mar. Apr. May June July Aug. Sept. Oct. Nov. Dec.

Dorsal (above)
warm brown and
somewhat
translucent

Ventral (below)
orange brown lines

round to oval yellow-
rimmed black
eyespots

173

Dorsal

Larva

Comments: The Dusted Skipper is a butterfly of open, dry habitats, preferring areas that have been fire-maintained or subject to some level of disturbance that supports its native host grasses. Although widespread throughout much of the East, populations are scarce in Ohio. They tend to be scattered and highly localized but are most definitely worth the effort to locate. This species may need state protection, as the southern populations have not been seen for a decade or more; it is now known only from two sites in Lucas County. An early-season species, it produces only a single spring flight. Males frequently perch on low vegetation.

Dusted Skipper
Atrytonopsis hianna

Family/Subfamily: Skippers (Hesperiidae)/
Banded Skippers (Hesperiinae)

Wingspan: 1.4–1.7" (3.6–4.3 cm)

Above: dark chocolate brown with small glassy forewing
spots

Below: dark brown with gray frosting toward outer margin; forewing has small white forewing spots near
apex; hindwing has tiny white spot near base; face is
white with black mask

Sexes: similar

Egg: yellow, laid singly on host leaves

Larva: gray, pinkish dorsally, with numerous cream hairs,
a brown anal segment; reddish purple head

Larval Host Plants: various grasses including Little
Bluestem and Big Bluestem

Habitat: dry habitats including oak savannas, barrens,
utility easements, brushy fields and prairies

Broods: single generation

Abundance: rare to uncommon; localized

Compare: Dun Skipper (pg. 139) has a rounder forewing
and lacks the small white basal spot on the hindwing
below.

Resident

Jan. Feb. Mar. Apr. May June July Aug. Sept. Oct. Nov. Dec.

Dorsal (above)
glassy white spots

Ventral (below)
dusted gray

single white spot

Dorsal

Larva

Comments: The Hoary Edge is named for its distinct frosty white (hoary) patch on the underside of the hindwing. Primarily a butterfly of dry, brushy sites and open woodlands, it regularly ventures into nearby disturbed sites and may at times show up in home gardens. Although widespread throughout much of the East, it tends to be highly localized and most often encountered as lone individuals. Adults have a low, strong flight and can be a challenge to follow. Males perch on low, protruding vegetation and aggressively investigate and chase passing insects.

Hoary Edge
Achalarus lyciades

Family/Subfamily: Skippers (Hesperiidae)/
Spread-wing Skippers (Pyrginae)

Wingspan: 1.40–1.75" (3.6–4.4 cm)

Above: brown with broad band of gold spots across
forewing and checkered fringe

Below: brown; forewing as above but muted; hindwing
mottled dark brown at base with distinct broad white
marginal patch

Sexes: similar

Egg: cream, laid singly on host leaves

Larva: dark green with a dark dorsal stripe, numerous
tiny pale yellow dots and a thin, brownish orange lateral stripe; black head

Larval Host Plants: primarily beggarweeds, but other
legumes including bush clovers may occasionally be
used

Habitat: open woodlands, forest edges and adjacent disturbed roadsides and brushy areas

Broods: two generations

Abundance: uncommon to occasional

Compare: Silver-spotted Skipper (pg. 195) is larger, has a
clear white median ventral hindwing patch and round,
stubby tail. Golden-banded Skipper (pg. 187) lacks
white patch on ventral hindwing.

Resident

Jan. Feb. Mar. Apr. May June July Aug. Sept. Oct. Nov. Dec.

male

Dorsal (above)
gold band

Ventral (below)
pale outer portion

outer half hoary
white

Male

Larva

Comments: Leonard's Skipper is a large, reddish brown
skipper with a distinctive white spot band on the hindwing below. A late season species, it produces a
single generation each year that emerges in mid to
late August and continues flying well into September.
Although common across much of its northern range,
it is seldom overly abundant in Ohio. Populations tend
to be scattered and somewhat localized. Nonetheless,
it can be fairly numerous when encountered. Adults
have a powerful, fast flight and tend to be quite wary
and difficult to closely approach even when feeding.

Leonard's Skipper
Hesperia leonardus

Family/Subfamily: Skippers (Hesperiidae)/ Banded Skippers (Hesperiinae)

Wingspan: 1.50–1.75" (3.8–4.4 cm)

Above: tawny orange with broad dark brown borders and several small orange spots; forewings elongated and pointed

Below: hindwing is reddish brown with a distinct row of cream white spots

Sexes: similar, although female is primarily brown with pale forewing spots

Egg: whitish green, laid singly on or near host leaves

Larva: olive green with a black head marked with cream

Larval Host Plants: a variety of grasses including bent-grass, panic grasses, and Poverty Oatgrass

Habitat: open, grassy areas including old fields, road-sides, wet meadows, woodland clearings and margins

Broods: single generation

Abundance: rare to occasional; localized

Compare: Indian Skipper (pg. 247) has a light orange hindwing with a pale yellow spot band on the ventral hindwing; flies in early summer.

Resident

Jan. Feb. Mar. Apr. May June July Aug. **Sept.** Oct. Nov. Dec.

Dorsal (above)
tawny orange scaling

broad dark brown borders

Ventral (below)
reddish brown hindwing

distinct row of cream white spots

179

Larva

Comments: The Ocola Skipper is a year-round resident of the Southeast but frequently wanders far outside of its normal range and is considered a rare stray to Ohio. Although superficially appearing quite dull, fresh individuals often have a noticeable purplish sheen to the ventral hindwings that is particularly lovely in the bright sunlight. The butterfly can be encountered in a wide range of open habitats from wet meadows and marshes to forest edges and suburban gardens. Adults have a fast, darting flight typically within a few feet of the ground.

Ocola Skipper
Panoquina ocola

Family/Subfamily: Skippers (Hesperiidae)/
Banded Skippers (Hesperiinae)

Wingspan: 1.50–1.75" (3.8–4.4 cm)

Above: forewings are long and slender with pale median spots

Below: brown with light veins and a subtle purple sheen; typically darker toward margin; often has faint post-median spot band

Sexes: similar

Egg: green, laid singly on host leaves

Larva: light green with yellow stripes and green head

Larval Host Plants: various grasses including Southern Cutgrass

Habitat: marshes, pond margins, forest edges, road-sides, old fields, utility easements and gardens

Broods: multiple generations where resident

Abundance: rare

Compare: unique

Stray

Jan. Feb. Mar. Apr. May June July Aug. Sept. Oct. Nov. Dec.

Dorsal (above)
ig, narrow forewing
pale spots

Ventral (below)
darker brown toward margin; often with faint spot band; subtle purple sheen on freshly emerged adults

181

Male

Female   Male   Larva

Comments: Juvenal's Duskywing is a widespread and common early spring species that can at times be exceedingly abundant. It is often confused with the similar Horace's Duskywing with which it often flies. At home in oak woodlands and other scrubby habitats, adults dart up and down sunlit trails and explore adjacent open sites with a quick, low flight. They frequently visit flowers or bask on bare ground with their wings spread. Males perch on low vegetation and actively pursue passing butterflies, often creating a whirl of activity. They frequently puddle at damp sand or gravel.

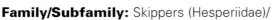

Juvenal's Duskywing
Erynnis juvenalis

Family/Subfamily: Skippers (Hesperiidae)/
Spread-wing Skippers (Pyrginae)

Wingspan: 1.5–1.9" (3.8–4.8 cm)

Above: dark brown; forewing has small cluster of tiny
clear spots near wingtip and one at end of cell, and is
heavily patterned with brown, gray, black and tan;
female has increased gray scaling and heavier pattern

Below: brown, lightening toward wing margin; hindwing
has two small, light spots along leading margin

Sexes: similar, although female is lighter and more heavily patterned with larger forewing spots

Egg: pale green, laid singly on host leaves

Larva: pale green with thin, light lateral stripe and reddish brown head; head capsule has a row of light
orange spots around the margin

Larval Host Plants: a wide variety of oaks including
White Oak

Habitat: oak woodlands and scrub, forest margins and
clearings, roadsides, utility easements and nearby
open areas

Broods: single generation

Abundance: occasional to abundant

Compare: Horace's Duskywing (pg. 167) lacks two light
spots on ventral hindwing and extensive gray scaling
on dorsal forewing.

Resident

Jan. Feb. Mar. Apr. May June July Aug. Sept. Oct. Nov. Dec.

male

Dorsal (above)
small glassy spots

glassy spot at end
of cell

heavy gray scaling

Ventral (below)
two round light spots
along leading margin

183

Ventral

Larva

Comments: The Little Wood Satyr is one of our most abundant and commonly encountered satyrs. A butterfly of shady woodlands and associated clearings and margins, it dances along the forest floor with a relatively slow, bobbing flight but can move rapidly if disturbed. Adults periodically perch on leaf litter or low vegetation with their wings partially open. Adults feed at sap flows, animal dung, rotting fungi and fermenting fruit and do not visit flowers.

Little Wood Satyr
Megisto cymela

Family/Subfamily: Brush-foots (Nymphalidae)/
Satyrs and Wood Nymphs (Satyrinae)

Wingspan: 1.5–1.9" (3.3–4.8 cm)

Above: brown; forewing has two prominent yellow-
rimmed eyespots; hindwing has one to three (usually
one is quite small) prominent yellow-rimmed eyespots

Below: light brown with two dark brown lines across
both wings; each wing has some pearly silver markings between two large, yellow-rimmed eyespots

Sexes: similar, although female has larger eyespots

Egg: green, laid singly on host leaves

Larva: brown with a dark dorsal stripe, brown lateral
dashes, two short stubby tails on the rear and two
small horns on the head

Larval Host Plants: various grasses bluegrass and
Orchardgrass

Habitat: open woodlands, forest clearings, woodland
margins and adjacent brushy areas

Broods: single generation

Abundance: common

Compare: Carolina Satyr (pg. 135) is smaller and lacks
eyespots on the wings above.

Resident

Jan. Feb. Mar. Apr. May June July Aug. Sept. Oct. Nov. Dec.

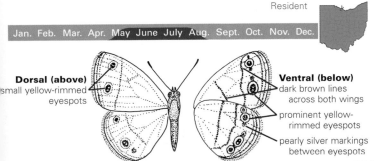

Dorsal (above)
small yellow-rimmed
eyespots

Ventral (below)
dark brown lines
across both wings

prominent yellow-
rimmed eyespots

pearly silver markings
between eyespots

185

Larva

Comments: Aptly named, this robust skipper had a distinct glassy yellow band across each forewing. A
denizen of damp, wooded areas along stream margins
or in shaded ravines, the Golden-banded Skipper is
generally quite elusive; most encounters are with solitary individuals. Adults have a somewhat slow but
highly erratic, darting flight close to the ground and can
be a challenge to follow. Males perch on low vegetation with their wings outstretched.

Golden-banded Skipper
Autochton cellus

Family/Subfamily: Skippers (Hesperiidae)/ Spread-wing Skippers (Pyrginae)

Wingspan: 1.5–2.0" (3.8–5.1 cm)

Above: brown; forewing has a golden yellow band across the center and a white spot below the apex; checkered fringe

Below: forewing is marked as above, but paler and mottled with faint dark brown spots; hindwing has two irregular dark brown bands and a light gray frosted patch along the margin

Sexes: similar

Egg: yellow, laid in short strings on host leaves

Larva: yellow green with a broad yellow lateral stripe, numerous small yellow dots; reddish brown head has two round yellow spots on the lower half

Larval Host Plants: Hog Peanut

Habitat: moist woodlands, forest margins, stream corridors, wetland edges and adjacent open areas

Broods: one to two generations

Abundance: rare to uncommon; highly localized

Compare: Hoary Edge (pg. 177) has a broad, dirty white patch along the margin of the ventral hindwing.

Resident

Jan. Feb. Mar. Apr. May June July Aug. Sept. Oct. Nov. Dec.

Dorsal (above)
white spots
r, glassy gold band
checkered fringe

Ventral (below)
mottled hindwing
gray frosting

187

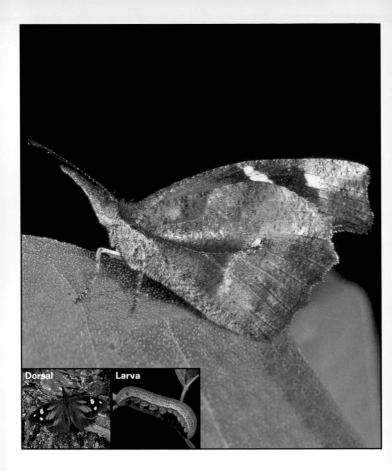

Dorsal

Larva

Comments: The American Snout gets its odd name
from the long labial palpi that resemble an elongated,
beak-like nose. This unique feature, combined with the
cryptic coloration of the wings beneath enhances the
butterfly's overall "dead leaf" appearance when it is at
rest. It is a permanent resident in the Deep South but
regularly moves north each year to temporarily colonize much of the U.S., including many portions of
Ohio. Nonetheless, the species is seldom overly
numerous within the state and typically found in close
association with stands of its larval host.

American Snout

Libytheana carinenta

Family/Subfamily: Brush-foots (Nymphalidae)/ Snouts (Libytheinae)

Wingspan: 1.6–1.9" (4.1–4.8 cm)

Above: brown with orange patches and white forewing spots; forewing apex is extended and squared off

Below: brown with orange basal forewing scaling and white spots; hindwing variable; plain gray brown or pinkish brown with heavy mottling

Sexes: similar

Egg: tiny white eggs laid in axils of host leaves

Larva: light green with numerous small yellow dots and yellow lateral stripe; rear portion has two small black lateral spots

Larval Host Plants: Common Hackberry, Sugarberry and Dwarf Hackberry

Habitat: rich, deciduous woodlands, stream corridors, swamps, forest edges, woodland clearings and adjacent open, brushy areas

Broods: multiple generations

Abundance: rare to uncommon; occasionally abundant

Compare: unique

Visitor

Jan. Feb. Mar. Apr. May June July Aug. Sept. Oct. Nov. Dec.

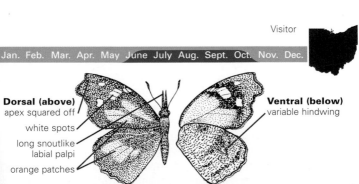

Dorsal (above)
apex squared off
white spots
long snoutlike labial palpi
orange patches

Ventral (below)
variable hindwing

189

Dorsal   Larva

Comments: The Appalachian Eyed Brown is a medium-sized brown butterfly. Often spotty and local, it prefers shaded habitats such as wooded swamps, moist grassy glades and forest margins. Adults have an erratic, bouncing flight and traverse low through wetland vegetation, stopping frequently to perch. Even when disturbed, they typically fly only a short distance before alighting within the vegetation again. As a result of their reclusive behavior, active colonies may be easily overlooked. Like most satyrs, the adults feed at sap flowers, fermenting fruit, animal dung or rotting fungi and not visit flowers.

Eyed Brown
Satyrodes eurydice

Family/Subfamily: Brush-foots (Nymphalidae)/ Satyrs and Wood Nymphs (Satyrinae)

Wingspan: 1.60–2.25" (4.1–5.7 cm)

Above: light brown with a submarginal row of small, solid black eyespots

Below: soft brown; forewing has straight, uniform row of 4 double-rimmed black eyespots; hindwing has row of 5 to 6 double-rimmed black eyespots with pale centers, bordered inwardly by dark, jagged postmedian line

Sexes: similar, although female is generally paler brown with larger eyespots

Egg: greenish white, laid singly on or near host leaves

Larva: light yellow-green with lateral red stripes and two short tails on the rear; two reddish horns on the head

Larval Host Plants: various sedges including Upright Sedge and Hairy Sedge

Habitat: marshes, sedge meadows, fens, roadside ditches and adjacent habitats

Broods: single generation

Abundance: occasional; localized

Compare: Appalachian Eyed Brown (pg. 193) has a smoother, more sinuous postmedian line on the ventral hindwing; the middle two eyespots on the ventral forewing are generally smaller than the one above or below.

Resident

Jan. Feb. Mar. Apr. May June July Aug. Sept. Oct. Nov. Dec.

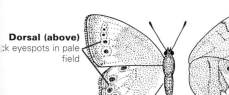

Dorsal (above)
black eyespots in pale field

Ventral (below)
roughly equal spots, touching

postmedian zig-zag line

Dorsal

Larva

Comments: Although called the Appalachian Brown, the range of this butterfly winds from northern Florida to southern Canada. In Ohio, it is reclusive, spotty and often highly localized within damp woodlands and shaded swamps. Like other wetland butterflies, it has suffered from continued loss of habitat due to urban development or agriculture. Adults have an erratic, low, bouncing flight and stop frequently to perch. Even when disturbed, they typically fly only a short distance before alighting again. Like most satyrs, the adults feed at sap flows, fermenting fruit, dung or rotting fungi and do not visit flowers.

Appalachian Brown
Satyrodes appalachia

Family/Subfamily: Brush-foots (Nymphalidae)/ Satyrs and Wood Nymphs (Satyrinae)

Wingspan: 1.90–2.25" (4.8–5.7 cm)

Above: light brown with small, solid black eyespots

Below: soft brown; forewing has a row of 4 double-rimmed black eyespots, the middle two generally smaller than one above or below; hindwing has row of 5 to 6 double-rimmed black eyespots with pale centers bordered inwardly by dark sinuous postmedian line

Sexes: similar, although female is generally paler brown with larger eyespots

Egg: greenish white, laid singly on or near host leaves

Larva: light green with narrow longitudinal yellow stripes, two short tails on the rear and two reddish horns on the head

Larval Host Plants: various grasses and sedges including Hairy Sedge, Upright Sedge and Fowl Mannagrass

Habitat: wooded swamps, moist, grassy glades, wet woodlands, stream corridors and forest margins

Broods: single generation

Abundance: rare to occasional; localized

Compare: Eyed Brown (pg. 191) has a more jagged brown postmedian line on the ventral hindwing and a fairly straight and uniform row of eyespots on the ventral forewing.

Resident

Jan. Feb. Mar. Apr. May June July Aug. Sept. Oct. Nov. Dec.

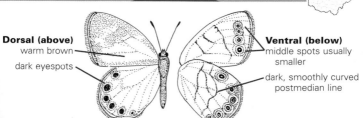

Dorsal (above)
warm brown
dark eyespots

Ventral (below)
middle spots usually smaller

dark, smoothly curved postmedian line

193

Dorsal

Larva

Comments: The Silver-spotted Skipper is a large, robust
butterfly named for the distinctive pure, silver-white
patch on the hindwing below. Adults have a powerful,
darting flight that offers a challenging pursuit. Luckily,
they are fond of flowers and readily pause to feed
where they can be closely observed.. They have a long
proboscis and can easily gain access to nectar from a
wide variety of blossoms. Males perch on shrubs or
overhanging branches and aggressively investigate
passing organisms. The colorful larvae construct individual shelters on the host by tying one or more leaves
together with silk.

Silver-spotted Skipper
Epargyreus clarus

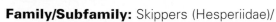

Family/Subfamily: Skippers (Hesperiidae)/ Spread-wing Skippers (Pyrginae)

Wingspan: 1.75–2.40" (4.4–6.1 cm)

Above: brown with median row of gold spots on forewing and checkered wing fringe; hindwing is tapered into small, rounded, lobe-like tail

Below: brown; forewing as above; hindwing has distinct, elongated clear silver-white patch in center

Sexes: similar

Egg: green, laid singly on host leaves

Larva: yellow-green with dark bands and reddish brown head

Larval Host Plants: wide variety of leguminous plants including Black Locust, wisteria, bush clover, False Indigo and Honey Locust

Habitat: forest edges, open woodlands, roadsides, utility easements, brushy fields, parks and gardens

Broods: two or more generations

Abundance: occasional to common

Compare: Hoary Edge (pg. 177) is smaller and has marginal white ventral hindwing patch. Golden-banded Skipper (pg. 187) lacks white patch on ventral hindwing.

Resident

Jan.	Feb.	Mar.	Apr.	May	June	July	Aug.	Sept.	Oct.	Nov.	Dec.

male

Dorsal (above)
elongated, narrow forewing
gold spots
checkered fringe
lobe-like tail

Ventral (below)
clear silver-white patch

Female

Ventral

Larva

Comments: The Common Buckeye is one of our most distinctive butterflies. The large eyespots help deflect attack away from the insect's vulnerable body or serve to startle would-be predators. It is fond of most open, sunny locations with low vegetation and may be an occasional garden visitor. Adults frequently alight on bare soil or gravel but are extremely wary and difficult to approach. Males readily establish territories and actively investigate most any passing insect. The flight of both sexes is rapid and low to the ground. It is a regular seasonal colonist of Ohio. As a result, it is fairly common in certain years and rare in others.

Common Buckeye
Junonia coenia

Family/Subfamily: Brush-foots (Nymphalidae)/
True Brush-foots (Nymphalinae)

Wingspan: 1.5–2.7" (3.8–6.9 cm)

Above: brown with prominent eyespots; forewing bears a distinct white patch and two small orange bars

Below: forewing has prominent white band; hindwings seasonally variable in color; summer forms are light brown with numerous pattern elements; cool-season forms are reddish brown with reduced markings

Sexes: similar, although female has broader wings and larger hindwing eyespots

Egg: dark green, laid singly on host leaves

Larva: black with lateral white stripes, orange patches and branched spines

Larval Host Plants: a wide variety of herbaceous plants several families (Acanthaceae, Verbenaceae, Scrophulariaceae, and Plantaginaceae) including toad-flax, false foxglove and plantain

Habitat: fields, pastures, roadsides, fallow agricultural land, gardens, open pineland, disturbed sites

Broods: multiple generations, overwinters as adult

Abundance: rare to occasional

Compare: unique

Visitor

Jan.	Feb.	Mar.	Apr.	May	June	July	Aug.	Sept.	Oct.	Nov.	Dec.

Dorsal (above)
white band that
surrounds
eyespot
orange bars
eyespots
orange band

Ventral (below)
seasonally variable

197

Dorsal

Larva

Comments: This is a large, somewhat reclusive butterfly of moist, shaded woodlands and stream corridors.
Colonies tend to be spotty and found in close association with patches of larval hosts; can be locally
numerous when encountered. Adults have a quick,
bobbing flight and maneuver close to the ground often
through dense forest undergrowth. They frequently
alight on low vegetation, tree trunks or on leaf litter.
They do not visit flowers but instead feed at sap
flows, rotting fruit, decaying vegetation, fungi and
dung. Unlike most butterflies, the adults are active on
overcast days and often fly late into the evening.

Northern Pearly Eye
Enodia anthedon

Family/Subfamily: Brush-foots (Nymphalidae)/ Satyrs and Wood Nymphs (Satyrinae)

Wingspan: 1.75–2.60" (4.3–6.6 cm)

Above: light brown with black eyespots in a pale field; hindwing has a slightly scalloped margin; antennal clubs are black at base

Below: brown with a violet cast; forewing has a straight row of four yellow-rimmed dark eyespots; hindwing has a cream band enclosing a row of yellow-rimmed dark eyespots with light highlights

Sexes: similar, although female generally has broader, more rounded wings and larger eyespots

Egg: greenish white, laid singly on host leaves

Larva: yellow green with narrow longitudinal yellow stripes, a dark green dorsal stripe, two short red-tipped tails on the rear and two reddish horns on the head

Larval Host Plants: various grasses including Whitegrass, Indian Woodoats, Tall Fresce, Silver Plumegrass, Bearded Shorthusk and Reed Canarygrss

Habitat: moist, shaded woodlands, stream corridors, marsh edges, fens and semi-open grassy areas along forest margins

Broods: two generations

Abundance: uncommon to occasional; localized

Compare: unique

Resident

Jan. Feb. Mar. Apr. May June July Aug. Sept. Oct. Nov. Dec.

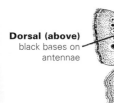

Dorsal (above)
black bases on antennae

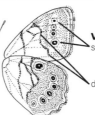

Ventral (below)
straight row of four eyespots; bottom two larger

dark, gently curved postmedian line

199

Male

Ventral

Larva

Comments: This lovely brown butterfly is named after its preferred larval host. A denizen of rich, shaded deciduous woodlands, it may occasionally show up in suburban yards or parks. Adults have a strong, rapid flight and often perch on sunlit leaves, overhanging branches or tree trunks along forest trails and wood-land edges. They are exceedingly pugnacious and inquisitive, and readily dart out investigate most any passing object, occasionally even landing on humans. Adults do not visit flowers but are drawn to sap flows or rotting fruit. Although often spotty and localized, it can be quite abundant when encountered.

Hackberry Butterfly
Asterocampa celtis

Family/Subfamily: Brush-foots (Nymphalidae)/ Emperors (Apaturinae)

Wingspan: 2.0–2.6" (5.1–6.6 cm)

Above: amber-brown with dark markings and borders; forewing bears several small white spots near the apex and a single submarginal black eyespot; hindwing has a postmedian row of dark spots

Below: as above with muted coloration; hindwing has postmedian row of yellow-rimmed black spots with blue green centers

Sexes: similar, although female has broader wings

Egg: cream-white, laid singly or in small clusters on leaves

Larva: light green with two narrow dorsal yellow stripe; mottled with small yellow spots; dark head bears two stubby, branched horns; rear end has a pair of short tails

Larval Host Plants: Common Hackberry, Sugarberry and Dwarf Hackberry

Habitat: moist, rich woodlands, forest margins and clearings, stream corridors, parks and yards

Broods: two generations

Abundance: occasional to common; localized

Compare: Tawny Emperor (pg. 205) is more orange-brown above and lacks white forewing spots and single forewing eyespot.

Resident

Jan. Feb. Mar. Apr. May June July Aug. Sept. Oct. Nov. Dec.

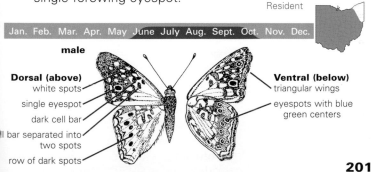

male

Dorsal (above)
white spots
single eyespot
dark cell bar
l bar separated into two spots
row of dark spots

Ventral (below)
triangular wings
eyespots with blue green centers

201

Dorsal

Larva

Comments: This is our largest wood nymph in Ohio. Adults have a low, relaxed flight and bob erratically among the vegetation, stopping frequently to alight low within the grasses. Unlike most satyrs, it is an opportunistic feeder and frequently visits flowers along with sap flows and fermenting fruit. The Common Wood Nymph is geographically variable and two forms or subspecies occur within the state. Populations with yellow forewing patches are common in southern regions of Ohio, whereas in more northern counties dark forewings predominate. Numerous intermediate forms can also be found.

Common Wood Nymph
Cercyonis pegala

Family/Subfamily: Brush-foots (Nymphalidae)/
Satyrs and Wood Nymphs (Satyrinae)

Wingspan: 1.8–2.8" (4.6–7.1 cm)

Above: brown; subspecies *alope* has two dark eyespots
containing white highlights surrounded by a large yellow patch on the forewing; subspecies *nephele* lacks
the yellow forewing patch

Below: brown with dark striations; subspecies *alope* has
a large yellow patch surrounding two dark eyespots
containing white highlights on the forewing; subspecies *nephele* lacks the yellow forewing patch and
has two yellow-rimmed two dark eyespots containing
white highlights

Sexes: similar, although female is paler and has larger
eyespots

Egg: cream, laid singly on host leaves

Larva: green with dark green dorsal stripe and light side
stripes

Larval Host Plants: various grasses including bluegrass, Poverty Oatgrass and Purpletop Grass

Habitat: wet meadows, grassy fields, open woodlands
and open, shrubby landscapes

Broods: single generation

Abundance: occasional to common

Compare: unique

Resident

Jan. Feb. Mar. Apr. May June July Aug. Sept. Oct. Nov. Dec.

form *alope*

Dorsal (above)
two large eyespots
yellow patch

Ventral (below)
geographically variable
throughout the U.S.

yellow-rimmed
eyespots

brown with black
striations

203

Male

Male   Female   Larva

Comments: The Tawny Emperor shares its affinity for rich woodlands with the Hackberry Butterfly. The two species are often found together but tend to be localized and seldom found far from stands of larval hosts. Adults are rapid, strong fliers, often difficult to closely approach. Males perch on sunlit leaves or on the sides of large trees along forest edges or clearings. They are pugnacious and inquisitive, and readily dart out to investigate virtually any passing object before returning to the same or nearby perch. The developing larvae remain together and feed communally through the first three instars before becoming more solitary.

Tawny Emperor
Asterocampa clyton

Family/Subfamily: Brush-foots (Nymphalidae)/ Emperors (Apaturinae)

Wingspan: 2.00–2.75" (5.1–7.0 cm)

Above: orange-brown with dark markings and borders; hindwing has a postmedian row of dark spots

Below: as above with muted gray-brown cast and small, dark hindwing eyespots

Sexes: similar, although female is much larger with broader, rounder wings

Egg: cream-white, laid in large pyramidal clusters on the underside of host leaves

Larva: light green with broad dorsal yellow stripes, narrow yellow lateral stripes and mottled with small yellow spots; head is green and bears two stubby, branched horns; rear end has a pair of short tails

Larval Host Plants: Common Hackberry, Sugarberry and Dwarf Hackberry

Habitat: rich, moist deciduous woodlands, forest clearings and margins, stream corridors, parks and yards

Broods: single generation

Abundance: uncommon to occasional; locally common

Compare: Hackberry Butterfly (pg. 201) is lighter brown with single black eyespot and white spots on forewing.

Resident

Jan. Feb. Mar. Apr. May June July Aug. Sept. Oct. Nov. Dec.

male

Dorsal (above)
narrow, triangular wings

no white spots

no black eyespot

two solid bars

Ventral (below)
muted pattern

small, dark eyespots

205

Ventral

Comments: This is a large, distinctive butterfly of northern forests. During years with population outbreaks, it periodically moves into more southern locations and should be considered a infrequent vagrant to Ohio. As a result, most sightings are of solitary individuals. Like other anglewings, Compton's Tortoiseshell has a quick, darting flight and is often quite way of close approach. Adults readily bask with their wings open in sunlit patches on gravel roads or in woodland clearings. They do not visit flowers but instead feed at fermenting fruit, dung, carrion and sap flows.

Compton Tortoiseshell
Nymphalis vaualbum

Family/Subfamily: Brush-foots (Nymphalidae)/
True Brush-foots (Nymphalinae)

Wingspan: 2.5–3.1" (6.4–7.9 cm)

Above: rusty brown with heavy black spots and golden
scaling toward outer margin; each wing bears a bright
white spot just below the apex; forewing apex is
extended and squared off; hindwing bears a single
short, stubby tail

Below: appears bark-like; heavily striated with gray and
brown; outer portion noticeably lighter than basal half

Sexes: similar

Egg: green, laid in clusters on host

Larva: light green with pale mottling and several rows of
lateral cream and dorsal black branched spines

Larval Host Plants: birch, willow and Quaking Aspen

Habitat: deciduous or mixed forests, clearings, woodland roads, forest edges and adjacent open areas

Broods: single generation

Abundance: rare to uncommon

Compare: unique

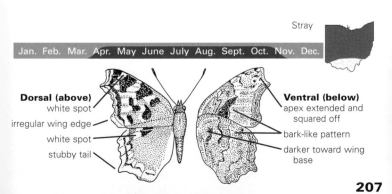

Stray

Jan. Feb. Mar. Apr. May June July Aug. Sept. Oct. Nov. Dec.

Dorsal (above)
white spot
irregular wing edge
white spot
stubby tail

Ventral (below)
apex extended and
squared off
bark-like pattern
darker toward wing
base

207

Male

Ventral Larva

Comments: With a wingspan approaching six inches, the Giant Swallowtail is one of the largest butterflies in North America. It is not highly tolerant of urban development. Populations tend to relatively small and in close association with its primary larval host. It is seldom overly abundant, and is particularly uncommon across eastern Ohio. Adults are fond of flowers and may occasionally wander into rural gardens. The larvae resemble bird droppings, an unappealing meal. If disturbed, the larva extends a red hornlike structure called an osmeterium from behind its head. The defensive gland omits a pungent odor and chemical irritant.

Giant Swallowtail
Papilio cresphontes

Family/Subfamily: Swallowtails (Papilionidae)/ Swallowtails (Papilioninae)

Wingspan: 4.5–5.5" (11.4–14.0 cm)

Above: chocolate brown with broad crossing bands of yellow spots; characteristic diagonal band extends from tip of forewing to base of abdomen; hindwing tail has yellow center

Below: cream yellow with brown markings and blue median hindwing band

Sexes: similar, although female is generally larger

Egg: amber-brown, laid singly on upperside of host leaves

Larva: brown with yellow and cream patches; resembles bird dropping

Larval Host Plants: Prickly Ash; Wafer Ash and various cultivated *Citrus* species may be used upon occasion

Habitat: open woodlands, pastures, forest margins, shrubby wetlands and adjacent open areas including pastures, roadsides, fields and rural gardens

Broods: multiple generations

Abundance: uncommon to occasional; localized

Compare: unique

Resident

Jan. Feb. Mar. Apr. May June July Aug. Sept. Oct. Nov. Dec.

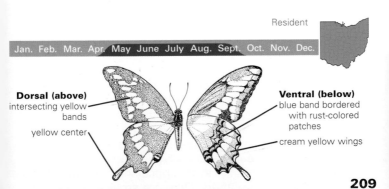

Dorsal (above)
intersecting yellow bands

yellow center

Ventral (below)
blue band bordered with rust-colored patches

cream yellow wings

209

Larva

Comments: The Red-banded Hairstreak has a rapid, erratic flight. Males typically perch on the sunlit leaves of small trees and shrubs (often on their hosts) and readily fly out to interact with other individuals, often spiraling high into the air before returning to a nearby perch. Unlike most other butterflies, female Red-banded Hairstreaks do not lay their eggs directly on the larval host. Instead, they land on the ground below appropriate hosts and deposit the small eggs singly on underside of dead, fallen leaves or other debris. The larvae feed primarily on this decaying plant material. Populations in southern Ohio are small and localized.

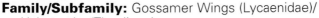

Red-banded Hairstreak
Calycopis cecrops

Family/Subfamily: Gossamer Wings (Lycaenidae)/
Hairstreaks (Theclinae)

Wingspan: 0.75–1.00" (1.9–2.5 cm)

Above: male is slate gray above with no markings;
female is slate gray with iridescent blue scaling on
hindwing; hindwing bears two short tails

Below: light gray with broad, red band edged outwardly
by a thin, wavy white line; blue scaling and a black
eyespot near tails

Sexes: similar, although female has blue scaling above

Egg: cream brown, laid on dead leaves below host

Larva: pinkish brown with numerous short hairs

Larval Host Plants: larvae are primarily detritivores,
feeding on dead leaves and other plant material below
certain shrubs or small trees including Winged Sumac
and Staghorn Sumac

Habitat: woodland edges and adjacent disturbed, brushy
areas, suburban gardens

Broods: two or more generations

Abundance: rare to occasional

Compare: Southern Hairstreak (pg. 117) lacks complete
red hindwing band.

Resident

Jan. Feb. Mar. Apr. May June July Aug. Sept. Oct. Nov. Dec.

Dorsal (above)
gray with varying
amount of blue
scaling

Ventral (below)
broad red band
edged outwardly
with black and
white

Male

Larva

Comments: This early-season blue is easily distinguished
from all other superficially similar azures by its dark,
charcoal gray-infused wings. Although now considered
a distinct species, individuals were previously thought
to be rare dark-colored forms of the Spring Azure. It
typically occurs in small, isolated colonies that are often
best discovered by first locating patches of its larval
host. Adults have a quick, directed flight usually close
to the ground. Males often join other azures at mud
puddles or stream banks to sip moisture. It typically
rests and feeds with its wings closed; dorsal color
shows in flight or while basking.

Dusky Azure
Celastrina nigra

Family/Subfamily: Gossamer Wings (Lycaenidae)/ Blues (Polyommatinae)

Wingspan: 0.75–1.25" (1.9–3.2 cm)

Above: male is uniform dark charcoal gray; female is pale gray blue with extensive, broad dark wing borders

Below: light gray with small black spots; hindwing has pale but prominent dark zigzag band along margin enclosing a row of small dark spots

Sexes: dissimilar; female is pale gray blue with extensive, broad dark wing borders, some white scaling, and distinct narrow dark cell-end bars

Egg: blue gray eggs laid singly young shoots, new leaves or flower buds of host

Larva: yellow green with pale lateral stripes

Larval Host Plants: goatsbeard or Bride's Feathers

Habitat: rich, shaded, deciduous woodlands, forest trails, woodland roads, shaded ravines, wooded ridgetops and stream corridors

Broods: single generation

Abundance: rare to uncommon; localized

Compare: Spring Azure (pg. 73) is blue above and has more extensive dark gray scaling below.

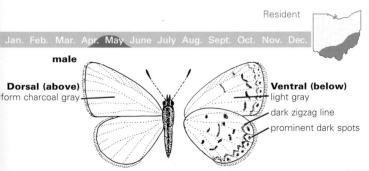

Resident

Jan. Feb. Mar. Apr. May June July Aug. Sept. Oct. Nov. Dec.

male

Dorsal (above)
form charcoal gray

Ventral (below)
light gray
dark zigzag line
prominent dark spots

213

Ventral

Larva

Comments: Relatively widespread and abundant, this small gray butterfly is one of our most commonly encountered hairstreaks. The adults are exceedingly fond of flowers and are regular visitors to home gardens or other more urban greenscapes. The small hair-like tails on the hindwing resemble antennae and presumably help deflect the attack of would-be predators away from the insect's vulnerable body. This charade, employed by many members of the family, is enhanced by the bright orange eyespots and converging lines on the wings below that draw attention to this unique false head feature.

Gray Hairstreak
Strymon melinus

Family/Subfamily: Gossamer Wings (Lycaenidae)/ Hairstreaks (Theclinae)

Wingspan: 1.0–1.5" (2.5–3.8 cm)

Above: slate gray with distinct reddish orange-capped black hindwing spot above tail

Below: light gray with black-and-white line across both wings (often with some orange); hindwing has reddish orange-capped black spot and blue scaling above tail

Sexes: similar; female larger with broader wings

Egg: light green, laid singly on flower buds or flowers of host

Larva: highly variable; bright green with lateral cream stripes to pinkish red

Larval Host Plants: wide variety of plants including Partridge Pea, beggarweeds, milk peas, milkvetch, lupine, bush clover, clover, vetch, mallow and Sida

Habitat: open, disturbed sites including roadsides, fallow agricultural land, pastures, old fields, suburban gardens; also woodland margins, prairies and rural meadows

Broods: multiple generations

Abundance: occasional to common

Compare: Southern Hairstreak (pg. 117) is brown on both wing surfaces. White M Hairstreak (pg. 83) is blue above with wide, black borders.

Resident

Jan. Feb. Mar. Apr. May June July Aug. Sept. Oct. Nov. Dec.

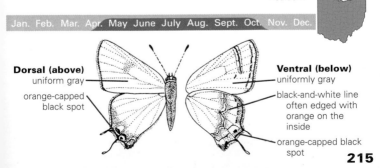

Dorsal (above)
uniform gray
orange-capped black spot

Ventral (below)
uniformly gray
black-and-white line often edged with orange on the inside
orange-capped black spot

215

Comments: This lovely gray hairstreak is restricted to wetland habitats or other moist areas that support willows. Although widespread across much of the Northeast and Great Lakes, the species tends to occur in relatively small, highly localized colonies but can be rather common when encountered. Adults have a quick, erratic flight and are most often observed at nearby moisture-loving flowers. They are particularly fond of milkweed blossoms.

Acadian Hairstreak
Satyrium acadica

Family/Subfamily: Gossamer Wings (Lycaenidae)/ Hairstreaks (Theclinae)

Wingspan: 1.10–1.45" (2.8–4.0 cm)

Above: brown with a small orange crescent-shaped hind-wing spot above a short tail

Below: uniform gray with a postmedian row of round, white-rimmed black spots; hindwing has a submarginal row of orange crescent-shaped spots and a orange-capped blue patch near the tail

Sexes: similar

Egg: white, laid singly on host twigs; eggs overwinter

Larva: green and white lateral stripe, pale white oblique dashes, and a darker green dorsal stripe edged in white

Larval Host Plants: various willows

Habitat: stream margins, pond edges, marshes, swamps, wet roadside ditches, depressions, bogs and moist meadows

Broods: single generation

Abundance: uncommon to occasional; localized

Compare: Edwards' Hairstreak (pg. 109) has gray-brown ventral wings and is typically found in more xeric (dry) habitats with oaks

Resident

Jan. Feb. Mar. Apr. May June July Aug. Sept. Oct. Nov. Dec.

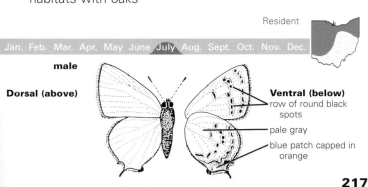

male

Dorsal (above)

Ventral (below)
row of round black spots

pale gray

blue patch capped in orange

217

Female

Female   Larva

Comments: This diminutive species is one of our scarcest resident butterflies. Only a small number of verified records exist from Ohio. The Early Hairstreak is a denizen of mixed hardwood forests where it frequents woodland roads or sunlit trails. The relative scarcity of adult sighting is likely due to their preference for spending time high in the canopy of mature host trees. As the larvae feed primarily on developing nuts, stands of young trees are not utilized. The adults periodically fly down from the treetops in search of nectar. They also regularly visit moist areas to sip moisture where they may occasionally be seen in numbers.

Early Hairstreak
Erora laeta

Family/Subfamily: Gossamer Wings (Lycaenidae)/ Hairstreaks (Theclinae)

Wingspan: 0.75–1.00" (1.9–2.5 cm)

Above: slate gray with blue scaling toward wing bases; tailless

Below: pale grayish green with a band of white-rimmed reddish orange spots across the wings; hindwing has a second row of smaller white-rimmed reddish orange spots along the outer margin

Sexes: dissimilar; female has increased iridescent blue scaling above with broad, dark gray borders

Egg: pale green laid singly on host leaves, buds, developing fruits and catkins

Larva: yellow green to rust brown with large reddish brown patches on the thorax and abdomen

Larval Host Plants: American Beech and Beaked Hazelnut

Habitat: hardwood forests and clearings, along woodland margins, sun dappled trails, stream corridors and roadsides

Broods: two generations

Abundance: rare

Compare: unique

Resident

| Jan. | Feb. | Mar. | Apr. | May | June | July | Aug. | Sept. | Oct. | Nov. | Dec. |

Dorsal (above)
gray with blue basal scaling

tailless

Ventral (below)
band of white-rimmed orange spots

grayish green hindwing

white-rimmed reddish orange spots

219

Larva

Comments: This diminutive green butterfly is arguably
our most beautiful hairstreak. It typically occurs in
spotty, highly localized colonies but can be somewhat
numerous when encountered. It is always found in
association with stands of Eastern Redcedar, its sole
larval host. This relationship is so intimate that the butterfly spends the majority of its adult life directly on
host trees, leaving only occasionally to nectar or possibly disperse to pioneer new colony sites. The adults
regularly perch high in the branches and may easily go
unnoticed. They are best discovered by gently tapping
the trunk or branches with a net handle or long pole.

Juniper Hairstreak
Callophrys gryneus

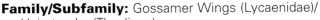

Family/Subfamily: Gossamer Wings (Lycaenidae)/ Hairstreaks (Theclinae)

Wingspan: 0.8–1.1" (2.0–2.8 cm)

Above: variable; unmarked brown to brown with extensive amber scaling; hindwing has two short tails; male has pale gray stigma on forewing

Below: bright olive green; forewing has a straight submarginal white band and reddish orange scaling along trailing edge; hindwing has two small white bars toward the base and an irregular white band across the middle that is edged on the inside with reddish brown

Sexes: similar, although female lacks pale forewing stigma

Egg: light green, laid singly on host

Larva: bright green with bold white dashes

Larval Host Plants: Eastern Redcedar

Habitat: old fields, forest edges, rocky outcrops, dry hillsides, bluffs, rural roadsides, farm windbreaks, old historical properties and even cemeteries

Broods: two generations

Abundance: rare to occasional; localized

Compare: unique

Resident

Jan. Feb. Mar. Apr. May June July Aug. Sept. Oct. Nov. Dec.

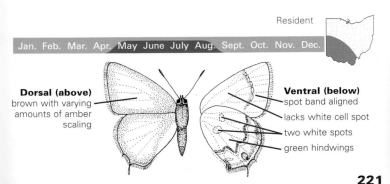

Dorsal (above)
brown with varying amounts of amber scaling

Ventral (below)
spot band aligned
lacks white cell spot
two white spots
green hindwings

221

Male | Female | Larva

Comments: The Least Skipper is a tiny, easy-to-identify
butterfly of wet, grassy areas throughout Ohio and
much of eastern North America. Highly adaptable to
human disturbance, it may be encountered in pristine
wetlands or damp drainage ditches, provided suitable
host grasses are present. Although somewhat local in
occurrence, it can at times be exceedingly abundant in
the right location. Adults have a low, weak flight and
flutter slowly through tall grasses pausing frequently to
perch. They regularly visit flowers but prefer low
plants with small blossoms.

Least Skipper
Ancyloxypha numitor

Family/Subfamily: Skippers (Hesperiidae)/ Banded Skippers (Hesperiinae)

Wingspan: 0.7–1.0" (1.8–2.5 cm)

Above: forewing orange-brown with dark border; hind-wing orange with dark border; rounded wings; male has a long, pointed abdomen

Below: forewing dark brown with orange border; hind-wing orange-gold

Sexes: similar, although female has a shorter abdomen

Egg: yellow, laid singly on or near host leaves

Larva: long and slender, light yellow-green with thin dark dorsal stripe and reddish brown head; head has numerous cream stripes

Larval Host Plants: various grasses including Rice Cutgrass, Giant Cutgrass, panic grass and cordgrass

Habitat: moist, grassy areas including roadside ditches, utility easements, wet meadows, pond edges and old fields

Broods: two or more generations

Abundance: occasional to abundant

Compare: European Skipper (pg. 225) is bright orange above, has more pointed forewings, and is not restricted to moist habitats.

Resident

Jan. Feb. Mar. Apr. May June July Aug. Sept. Oct. Nov. Dec.

male   rounded wings

Dorsal (above)
rounded wings
orange
heavy dark margin

Ventral (below)
dark brown
uniform golden orange

223

Ventral

Larva

Comments: This diminutive electric orange butterfly is a
regular sight in open, grassy areas throughout Ohio.
The European Skipper also adapts well to more urban
locations, frequently showing up in suburban gardens,
parks and vacant lots. As its name implies, the species
was accidentally introduced into Ontario, Canada from
Europe in 1910 and continues to expand its range.
Although superficially similar to the Least Skipper, it is
less restricted to moist habitats. Adults maneuver
close to the ground among grassy vegetation with a
slow and somewhat erratic flight.

European Skipper
Thymelicus lineola

Family/Subfamily: Skippers (Hesperiidae)/
Banded Skippers (Hesperiinae)

Wingspan: 0.9–1.1" (2.3–2.8 cm)

Above: bronzy orange wings with dark brown borders;
veins are darkened toward the outer wing margins

Below: unmarked orange

Sexes: similar, although female is somewhat darker with
veins darkened to base

Egg: white, laid on host stems

Larva: pale green with a darker green dorsal stripe,
white lateral stripes and a greenish tan head marked
with two vertical cream stripes on the face

Larval Host Plants: various grasses including Timothy
Grass, Orchardgrass, Common Velvetgrass and bentgrass

Habitat: open, grassy areas including roadsides, utility
easements, old fields, wet meadows, prairies, stream
margins, pastures, parks and gardens

Broods: single generation

Abundance: occasional to common; localized

Compare: Least Skipper (pg. 223) has more rounded
wings, solid dark dorsal borders, and produces multiple generations.

Resident

Jan. Feb. Mar. Apr. May June July Aug. Sept. Oct. Nov. Dec.

Dorsal (above)
dark brown
borders

veins darker
toward outer
margins

bronzy orange

Ventral (below)
unmarked orange

Ventral

Comments: Despite its name, the Northern Metalmark's range also extends well southward into Kentucky and Oklahoma. Although widespread across much of Ohio, the species is a rare resident of dry woodland openings and is typically encountered in small, highly localized populations that are closely associated with patches of its sole larval host. Adults have a low, weak flight and regularly alight on vegetation with their wings spread. Both sexes are fond of flowers and can readily be observed while nectaring.

Northern Metalmark
Calephelis borealis

Family/Subfamily: Gossamer Wings (Lycaenidae)/ Metalmarks (Riodininae)

Wingspan: 0.9–1.2" (2.3–3.0 cm)

Above: reddish brown with numerous small dark markings, a darker broad median band, and two narrow, metallic gray bands along the outer edge of the wings

Below: marked similarly to upper surface but brighter orange

Sexes: similar, although female has broader, more rounded wings

Egg: reddish, laid singly on the underside of host leaves

Larva: greenish with tiny black dots; covered in long whitish hairs

Larval Host Plants: Round-leaf Ragwort

Habitat: dry, open woodlands and adjacent clearings

Broods: single generation

Abundance: rare; localized

Compare: Swamp Metalmark (pg. 229) lacks the broad dark median band across the wings and inhabits alkaline wetlands.

Resident

| Jan. | Feb. | Mar. | Apr. | May | June | July | Aug. | Sept. | Oct. | Nov. | Dec. |

male

Dorsal (above)
forewing strongly convex

dark median band

Ventral (below)
bright orange

rows of metallic spots

Ventral

Larva

Comments: This dainty orange butterfly is restricted entirely to alkaline wetlands that support its sole larval host. Much of the species' habitat in the Upper Midwest has been lost due to urban development, agriculture or habitat alteration. It has not been seen in Ohio since 1988, and is now considered to be extirpated. The adults scurry low to the ground among grassy vegetation and frequently stop to perch on leaves with their wings held wide open. During periods of inclement weather or if disturbed, they often fly quickly and land out of sight on the underside of large, broad leaves.

Swamp Metalmark
Calephelis muticum

Family/Subfamily: Gossamer Wings (Lycaenidae)/ Metalmarks (Riodininae)

Wingspan: 0.9–1.2" (2.3–3.0 cm)

Above: reddish brown with numerous small dark markings and two narrow, metallic gray bands along the outer edge of the wings

Below: marked similarly to upper surface but brighter orange

Sexes: similar, although female has broader, more rounded wings

Egg: reddish, laid singly on the underside of host leaves

Larva: green with tiny black dots; covered in long whitish hairs

Larval Host Plants: Swamp Thistle

Habitat: wet meadows and alkaline fens

Broods: single generation

Abundance: extirpated

Compare: Northern Metalmark (pg. 227) has a broad dark median band across the wings and inhabits dry, open woodlands.

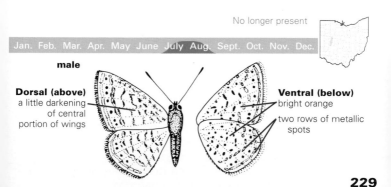

No longer present

Jan. Feb. Mar. Apr. May June July Aug. Sept. Oct. Nov. Dec.

male

Dorsal (above)
a little darkening of central portion of wings

Ventral (below)
bright orange

two rows of metallic spots

229

Male pg. 105   Larva

Comments: Living up to its name, male Purplish
Coppers have an iridescent purple sheen on the wings
above that is stunning when seen in sunlight. Primarily
relegated to moist areas, colonies tend to be small and
highly localized. Expanding agricultural activities, urban
development and habitat degradation have severely
restricted the butterfly's range and population in Ohio.
Now severely imperiled, it is one of seven butterflies
listed by the Ohio DNR as endangered. It is being bred
and reintroduced by the Toledo Zoological Gardens.
Males perch low on grasses or other vegetation with
their wings partially open to await passing females.

Purplish Copper
Lycaena helloides

Family/Subfamily: Gossamer Wings (Lycaenidae)/ Coppers (Lycaeninae)

Wingspan: 1.0–1.2" (2.5–3.0 cm)

Above: male is brown with a strong purplish iridescence and scattered black; female is primarily orange with scattered black spots and broad brown borders; hindwing has a broad scalloped orange submarginal band

Below: forewing is orange with scattered black spots and a purplish brown apex and outer margin; hindwing purplish brown with small black spots and a narrow, irregular reddish orange submarginal line

Sexes: dissimilar; female has increased orange scaling on both wings

Egg: greenish white, laid singly on the host

Larva: green with several yellow stripes

Larval Host Plants: knotweed and dock

Habitat: open, moist habitats including wet meadows, stream margins, roadside ditches, pond margins, fallow agricultural land and marshes

Broods: two or more generations

Abundance: rare; localized

Compare: American (pg. 237) and Bronze (pg. 159) Coppers have silvery gray ventral hindwings. Bronze also has a wide reddish orange submarginal band.

Resident

Jan. Feb. Mar. Apr. May June July Aug. Sept. Oct. Nov. Dec.

male

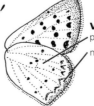

Dorsal (above)
iridescent purple/brown (both wings)

zig-zag orange outer margin

Ventral (below)
purplish brown

narrow orange submarginal line

231

Male

Male Female Larva

Comments: The Long Dash is a locally common butterfly of open, moist habitats. Its unusual name makes reference to the narrow dark spot near the tip of the forewing that appears to elongate the black stigma. The energetic adults scurry over the top of wetland vegetation with a rapid, erratic flight. Males perch low to the ground to await passing females. Both sexes may wander into nearby drier habitat sites in search of available nectar sources.

Long Dash
Polites mystic

Family/Subfamily: Skippers (Hesperiidae)/
Banded Skippers (Hesperiinae)

Wingspan: 1.00–1.25" (2.5–3.2 cm)

Above: yellow-orange with broad, dark brown borders;
ale has a broad, long black forewing stigma below an
elongated dark subapical spot

Below: hindwing is reddish brown with a broad yellow
postmedian band and small basal spot

Sexes: dissimilar; female has reduced tawny-orange scaling and dark brown wing bases

Egg: pale green, laid singly on host

Larva: dark brown with fine white mottling and a black
dorsal stripe; black head

Larval Host Plants: various gasses including bluegrass

Habitat: swamps, marshes, wet grassy meadows, fens,
roadside ditches, woodland margins and other open
wetland sites

Abundance: uncommon to occasional; locally abundant

Broods: single generation

Compare: Peck's Skipper (pg. 115) is smaller and has
yellow postmedian band on hindwing below with elongated central spot. Indian Skipper (pg. 247) has a
narrower pale postmedian band on the hindwing
below and is found in drier habitats.

Resident

Jan. Feb. Mar. Apr. May June July Aug. Sept. Oct. Nov. Dec.

male

Dorsal (above)
long stigma
slightly curved

Ventral (below)
small basal spot

band of equal-sized
yellow spots

Male

Female Male Larva

Comments: The Fiery Skipper is abundant in most open, sunny locations throughout the Deep South. A prolific colonizer, it regularly expands its range northward each summer, often temporarily colonizing much of the East before freezing back with the arrival of cold weather. Adults have a rapid, darting flight but often stop to perch on low vegetation. They are exceedingly fond of flowers and readily congregate at available blossoms. They have a strong preference for colorful composites. The larvae utilize a variety of grasses including many commonly planted for southern lawns. As a result, the butterfly is often mentioned as a minor turf pest.

Fiery Skipper
Hylephila phyleus

Family/Subfamily: Skippers (Hesperiidae)/
Banded Skippers (Hesperiinae)

Wingspan: 1.00–1.25" (2.5–3.2 cm)

Above: elongated wings; male is golden orange with
jagged black border and black stigma; female is tawny
orange with dark brown bands

Below: hindwing golden orange in male or orange brown
in female with tiny dark brown spots

Sexes: dissimilar; female darker with reduced orange
markings and larger hindwing spots

Egg: whitish green, laid singly on host leaves

Larva: greenish brown with thin, dark brown dorsal
stripe and black head

Larval Host Plants: a variety of grasses including
Bermuda Grass, crabgrass, bentgrass and St.
Augustine Grass

Habitat: open, grassy areas including old fields, roadsides, vacant lots, open woodlands, forest edges,
parks, lawns and gardens

Broods: multiple generations where resident

Abundance: rare to occasional

Compare: Sachem (pg. 245) lacks small scattered dark
spots on the hindwing below.

Visitor

| Jan. | Feb. | Mar. | Apr. | May | June | July | Aug. | Sept. | Oct. | Nov. | Dec. |

male

Dorsal (above)
orange

jagged black
margins

Ventral (below)
elongated wings

small scattered dark
spots

235

Ventral

Larva

Comments: Although called the American Copper, some
suggest that the eastern populations of the butterfly
may actually be the result of historical introductions
from Europe. This argument is fueled by the species'
unique preference for open, disturbed habitats and primary use of a weedy, non-native larval host. It tends to
occur in widespread and highly localized colonies, but
is often fairly common when encountered. The adults
frequently perch on bare soil or on low vegetation with
the wings held in a characteristic, partially open posture. When first seen in bright sunlight, there remains
little doubt as to why the butterfly is called a copper!

American Copper
Lycaena phlaeas

Family/Subfamily: Gossamer Wings (Lycaenidae)/ Coppers (Lycaeninae)

Wingspan: 0.9–1.4" (2.3–3.6 cm)

Above: bright red orange forewings with black spots and dark borders; hindwing is gray with wide scalloped submarginal orange band subtended by black spots along outer margin

Below: forewing is pale orange with prominent white-rimmed black spots and light gray apex and outer margin; hindwing is silvery gray with small white-rimmed black spots and narrow, irregular reddish orange line along outer margin

Sexes: similar, although female is larger and has more rounded wings

Egg: pale greenish white, laid singly host stems or leaves

Larva: variable; yellow green to rose, often with a narrow lateral stripe

Larval Host Plants: Sheep Sorrel and Curly Dock

Habitat: open, sunny areas including old fields, pastures, roadsides, meadows and alfalfa or clover fields

Broods: three or more generations

Abundance: uncommon to locally common

Compare: Bronze Copper (pg. 253) is larger and has a broad reddish orange submarginal band on the ventral hindwing.

Resident

Jan. Feb. Mar. Apr. May June July Aug. Sept. Oct. Nov. Dec.

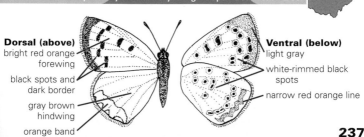

Dorsal (above)
bright red orange forewing

black spots and dark border

gray brown hindwing

orange band

Ventral (below)
light gray

white-rimmed black spots

narrow red orange line

Larva

Comments: Unique in both appearance and behavior, the Harvester is the only North American butterfly with carnivorous larvae. A denizen of woodland habitats, the species tends to be found in small, localized colonies in close association with populations of its host aphids. Males are regularly encountered perching on sunlit leaves or imbibing moisture at damp ground along forest trails, unpaved roads or stream margins. The butterfly has a fast, erratic flight and can be a challenge to follow. Adults feed primarily on sugary aphid honeydew and rarely, if ever, visit flowers.

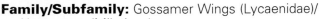

Harvester
Feniseca tarquinius

Family/Subfamily: Gossamer Wings (Lycaenidae)/
Harvesters (Miletinae)

Wingspan: 1.1–1.3" (2.8–3.3 cm)

Above: orange with brown to black spots, patches and
borders

Below: brown; forewing has orange central scaling and
several dark patches outlined in white; hindwing has
numerous dark spots outlined in white and silver scaling toward base

Sexes: similar

Egg: greenish white, laid singly among aphid colonies

Larva: gray with whitish yellow bumps bordered with
brown along top, reddish brown lateral stripes and
long gray hairs

Larval Host Plants: does not feed on plant material;
carnivorous on woolly aphids

Habitat: forest edges, stream corridors, swamp margins,
moist woodlands and associated clearings, trails and
roads

Broods: multiple generations

Abundance: rare to occasional; often highly localized

Compare: unique

Resident

Jan. Feb. Mar. Apr. May June July Aug. Sept. Oct. Nov. Dec.

female

Dorsal (above)
orange with black
border and spots

Ventral (below)
reddish brown with
silver scaling and
numerous brown
spots outlined in
white

Female

Ventral

Larva

Comments: The Delaware Skipper is an orange butterfly with elongated, somewhat pointed forewings. The wings beneath are an immaculate golden yellow. Found primarily in a variety of moist, grassy habitats from damp meadows to marshes, the butterfly frequently finds is way into more human-disturbed locations including suburban yards. Although widespread, it is seldom overly abundant and often somewhat local. Adults have a quick, darting flight and are fond of flowers. Males perch on low leaves and grasses and make frequent exploratory flights.

Delaware Skipper
Anatrytone logan

Family/Subfamily: Skippers (Hesperiidae)/ Banded Skippers (Hesperiinae)

Wingspan: 1.0–1.4" (2.5–3.6 cm)

Above: orange with dark borders and veins; forewings are elongated and somewhat pointed; male has a small black cell-end bar on forewing; female has brown scaling in forewing cell, wider borders, and forewing cell-end bar is larger

Below: unmarked golden orange

Sexes: similar, although female darker with reduced orange coloration

Egg: white, laid singly on host leaves

Larva: bluish white with dark tubercles and a black-and-white head

Larval Host Plants: various grasses including bluestems, Silver Plumegrass and Switchgrass

Habitat: open woodlands, forest edges, prairies, fens, roadsides, pastures, wetland edges, retention ponds, utility easements and old fields

Broods: single generation

Abundance: uncommon to occasional

Compare: European Skipper (pg. 225) is smaller, has shorter antennae and lacks black cell-end bar on the forewing above.

Resident

Jan. Feb. Mar. Apr. May June July Aug. Sept. Oct. Nov. Dec.

male

Dorsal (above)
dark border
in black cell-end bar
dark veins

Ventral (below)
unmarked golden orange

241

Male

Female pg. 127 | Male | Female | Larva

Comments: The Zabulon Skipper is strikingly dimorphic with bright orange males and purplish brown females. A denizen of wooded habitats, the butterfly is most often encountered in dappled sunlit patches along forest trails or clearings. Nonetheless, individuals will wander into nearby, more open landscapes in search of available nectar resources. The pugnacious males perch on branches around head-height to await passing mates and aggressively fly out to engage rival males before returning to the same or nearby perch moments later. Females generally prefer to remain within the confines of shadier locales.

Zabulon Skipper
Poanes zabulon

Family/Subfamily: Skippers (Hesperiidae)/
Banded Skippers (Hesperiinae)

Wingspan: 1.0–1.4" (2.5–3.6 cm)

Above: male is golden orange with dark brown borders
and small brown spot near forewing apex; female is
dark brown with band of cream spots across forewing

Below: male hindwing yellow with a brown base enclosing a yellow spot; female is dark brown with small
light subapical spots, lavender scaling on wing margins, and white bar along leading margin of hindwing

Sexes: dissimilar, female brown with little orange color

Egg: pale green, laid singly on host leaves

Larva: tan with dark dorsal stripe, white lateral stripe and
short, light-colored hairs; reddish brown head

Larval Host Plants: various grasses including
Purpletop Grass, Whitegrass and lovegrass

Habitat: open woodlands, forest margins and roadsides,
shrubby fields, stream corridors, utility easements and
adjacent open landscapes

Broods: two generations

Abundance: uncommon to occasional

Compare: Sachem (pg. 245) is similar to male Zabulon
Skipper, but dark hindwing base does not enclose yellow patch.

Resident

Jan. Feb. Mar. Apr. May June July Aug. Sept. Oct. Nov. Dec.

male

Dorsal (above)
dark spot

narrow black cell
end bar

golden orange

clear golden
orange

Ventral (below)
dark base encloses
yellow spot

yellow with darker
spots

243

Male

Female pg. 133   Male   Female   Larva

Comments: The Sachem has an affinity for just about any open, sunny habitat. This southern butterfly regularly wanders northward and may periodically colonize portions of Ohio. Temporary breeding populations are sporadic, but can at times reach high densities. Adults have a very rapid, darting flight that is usually low to the ground. Exceedingly fond of flowers, they often form a circus of activity with several individuals pausing briefly to perch or nectar before one flies up and disturbs the others.

Sachem
Atalopedes campestris

Family/Subfamily: Skippers (Hesperiidae)/
Banded Skippers (Hesperiinae)

Wingspan: 1.0–1.5" (2.5–3.8 cm)

Above: elongated wings; male is golden orange with
brown borders and large, black stigma; female is dark
brown with golden markings in wing centers; forewing
has black median spot and several semitransparent
spots

Below: variable; hindwing golden brown in male, brown
in female with pale postmedian patch or band of spots

Sexes: dissimilar; female darker with semitransparent
forewing spots and reduced orange markings

Egg: white, laid singly on host leaves

Larva: greenish brown with thin, dark dorsal stripe and
black head

Larval Host Plants: various grasses including Bermuda
Grass and crabgrass

Habitat: open, disturbed areas including old fields, pastures, roadsides, parks, lawns and gardens

Broods: one or more generations

Abundance: rare to occasional

Compare: Fiery Skipper (pg. 235) has small dark spots
on the hindwing below.

Visitor

| Jan. | Feb. | Mar. | Apr. | May | June | July | Aug. | Sept. | Oct. | Nov. | Dec. |

male

Dorsal (above)
large rectangular
stigma

golden orange

Ventral (below)
faint dark spot along
trailing margin

large pale patch

245

Ventral

Female

Larva

Comments: Although widespread throughout the
Northeast, the range of this lovely tawny-orange skipper is generally restricted to eastern portions of Ohio.
Colonies are generally spotty, low density and local in
occurrence. The Indian Skipper has never been overly
common in Ohio; most sightings are of single adults
and only one or two active sites are known today. A
highly active butterfly, adults have a very rapid flight
and nervously pause for a moment at an available
early-season blossom before darting off again.

Indian Skipper
Hesperia sassacus

Family/Subfamily: Skippers (Hesperiidae)/
Banded Skippers (Hesperiinae)

Wingspan: 1.2–1.4" (3.0–3.6 cm)

Above: bright orange with wide, somewhat jagged, dark
brown borders

Below: hindwing is tawny orange with a pale golden
orange spot band through center; middle spot dis-
placed outward toward margin

Sexes: similar, although female has broader dark borders,
larger, paler yellow orange spot bands and reduced
orange scaling

Egg: whitish green, laid singly on host leaves or stems

Larva: dark brown, often with lighter mottling and a
round black head

Larval Host Plants: various grasses including Little
Bluestem, panic grasses, Poverty Oatgrass, bluegrass
and Red Fescue

Habitat: woodland clearings and margins, pastures, old
brushy fields and forest meadows

Broods: single generation

Abundance: rare to occasional; localized

Compare: Leonard's Skipper (pg. 179) has reddish
brown ventral hindwings with a bold white postmedian
spot band and flies in late summer.

Resident

Jan. Feb. Mar. Apr. May June July Aug. Sept. Oct. Nov. Dec.

male

Dorsal (above)
dark, sharply
defined borders

Ventral (below)
pale spot band with
center spot offset
toward outer margin

247

Male

Male ventral Female Female ventral Larva

Comments: This is our most widespread and abundant
crescent. At home in most open, sunny landscapes
with nearby available hosts, it frequents old fields and
rural pastures as well as gardens and urban parks. It is
seasonally variable with spring and fall (short-day
forms) individuals being darker and more heavily patterned on the hindwings below. It is an opportunistic
breeder, continually producing new generations as
long as favorable conditions allow. Adults have a rapid,
erratic flight. Males perch on low vegetation with
wings outstretched and frequently patrol for females.
Freshly emerged males often gather at moist ground.

Pearl Crescent
Phyciodes tharos

Family/Subfamily: Brush-foots (Nymphalidae)/
True Brush-foots (Nymphalinae)

Wingspan: 1.25–1.60" (3.2–4.1 cm)

Above: orange with dark bands, spots and wing borders

Below: seasonally variable; light brownish orange with
brown markings; winter-form has increased dark coloration and pattern elements

Sexes: similar, although female is paler orange with
increased black markings

Egg: green, laid in clusters on underside of host leaves

Larva: dark brown to charcoal with lateral cream stripes
and numerous short, branched spines

Larval Host Plants: various asters including Frost
Aster, Smooth Blue Aster and Bushy Aster

Habitat: virtually any open, sunny habitat including roadsides, old fields, utility easements, forest edges,
prairies, meadows, pastures and gardens

Broods: multiple generations

Abundance: occasional to abundant

Compare: Northern Crescent (pg. 269) has larger, more
open orange areas on the hindwing above and orange
antennal clubs; frequents semi-open moist woodlands.
Silvery Checkerspot (pg. 267) is larger with a submarginal row of white-centered, square spots on
the hindwing above.   Resident

Jan. Feb. Mar. Apr. May June July Aug. Sept. Oct. Nov. Dec.

male

Dorsal (above)
fine black lines

wide black borders

Ventral (below)
yellow-orange with
light reticulations

pale crescent in dark
marginal patch

seasonally variable

249

Male

Larva

Comments: Generally an uncommon butterfly throughout its limited Midwestern range, the Black Dash is restricted to marshes, wet meadows and other open wetlands with abundant sedge. As a result, populations tend to be small and highly localized to suitable habitat areas. The adults are swift on the wing but are easily observed when feeding at nearby wetland wildflowers. Males perch like sentinels on tall grasses watching keenly for passing females and readily fly out to engage intruders.

Black Dash
Euphyes conspicua

Family/Subfamily: Skippers (Hesperiidae)/
Banded Skippers (Hesperiinae)

Wingspan: 1.25–1.60" (3.2–4.1 cm)

Above: golden-orange with broad, dark brown borders;
male has a broad black stigma

Below: hindwing orange-brown with a broad yellow postmedian patch

Sexes: dissimilar; female is primarily dark brown with
pale yellow forewing spots

Egg: laid singly on host

Larva: green with fine white mottling; brown head
marked with cream lines around the margin and a
black oval on the forehead

Larval Host Plants: various sedges including Upright
Sedge

Habitat: marshes, wet grassy meadows, fens, roadside
ditches, bogs, woodland margins and other open wetland sites

Abundance: uncommon to occasional; localized

Broods: single generation

Compare: Peck's Skipper (pg. 115) is smaller and has
yellow basal spots on the hindwing below. Dion
Skipper (pg. 257) is larger and has a long pale ray
through the hindwing without adjacent
postmedian spots.   Resident

Jan. Feb. Mar. Apr. May June July Aug. Sept. Oct. Nov. Dec.

male

Dorsal (above)
heavy stigma
dark brown
borders
orange

Ventral (below)
red-brown hindwing
curved yellow patch

Female

Male pg. 159   Ventral   Larva

Comments: This sexually dimorphic species is our largest copper. Although primarily restricted to moist areas where its weedy larval hosts occur, it frequently wanders into nearby drier habitats in search of nectar. The Bronze Copper tends to occur in small, highly localized colonies but can be rather numerous when encountered. Like many other wetland species, it has suffered from the loss or degradation of available habitat. Males perch low on grasses or other vegetation with their wings partially open to await passing females.

Bronze Copper
Lycaena hyllus

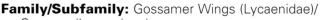

Family/Subfamily: Gossamer Wings (Lycaenidae)/ Coppers (Lycaeninae)

Wingspan: 1.25–1.65" (3.2–4.2 cm)

Above: male is brown with a purplish iridescence and a broad orange submarginal band containing black spots on the hindwing; female has light orange forewings with scattered black spots and a broad brown border; hindwing is purplish brown with a broad orange submarginal band containing black spots

Below: scattered white-rimmed black spots on both wings; forewing is orange with silvery gray apex and margin; hindwing is silvery gray with broad orange submarginal band containing black spots

Sexes: dissimilar; female is larger with rounder wings and increased orange scaling on the dorsal forewing

Egg: whitish, laid singly on host leaves or stems

Larva: yellow-green with a darker green dorsal stripe

Larval Host Plants: knotweed, Curly Dock, Water Dock

Habitat: open, moist habitats including fens, wet meadows and marshes; also adjacent clover fields

Broods: two or more generations

Abundance: uncommon to locally common

Compare: American (pg. 237) and Purplish (pg. 105) Coppers are smaller and have a narrow, reddish orange submarginal line on ventral hindwing.

Resident

Jan. Feb. Mar. Apr. May June July Aug. Sept. Oct. Nov. Dec.

male

Dorsal (above)
iridescent purple/brown above

orange band

Ventral (below)
pale orange forewing

small spots

off white hindwing

orange submarginal band

253

Male   Female   Female "Pocahontas" pg. 165   Larva

Comments: This small woodland skipper has a single spring flight. Males perch on sunlit leaves and aggressively dart out at other passing butterflies. They may also frequently be encountered at wet earth along forested roads or trails. Although preferring shadier conditions, both sexes will venture into nearby open areas to nectar at early-season blossoms. Female Hobomoks produce two distinct forms. The lighter form resembles the male and the darker form "Pocahontas" is superficially similar to Zabulon Skipper females. Larvae construct individual leaf shelters on the host. Larvae overwinter.

Hobomok Skipper
Poanes hobomok

Family/Subfamily: Skippers (Hesperiidae)/
Banded Skippers (Hesperiinae)

Wingspan: 1.4–1.6" (3.6–4.1 cm)

Above: golden orange with irregular dark brown borders
and a narrow black cell-end bar on the forewing

Below: purplish brown with a broad yellow orange patch
through the hindwing

Sexes: dissimilar; female has two forms. Normal form
resembles male but has reduced orange scaling above.
"Pocahontas" form is dark brown above with pale
forewing spots; hindwing is purplish brown below with
faint band and violet gray frosting along outer margin.

Egg: white, laid singly on host leaves

Larva: brown green with numerous short, light-colored
hairs; round, brown head

Larval Host Plants: various grasses including Little
Bluestem, panic grasses, Poverty Oatgrass, bluegrass
and Rice Cutgrass

Habitat: open woodlands, forest edges, clearings and
trails, roadsides and along forested stream margins

Broods: single generation

Abundance: occasional to common

Compare: Zabulon (pg. 255) and Peck's (pg. 115)
Skippers have yellow basal scaling on ventral hindwing. Resident

Jan. Feb. Mar. Apr. May June July Aug. Sept. Oct. Nov. Dec.

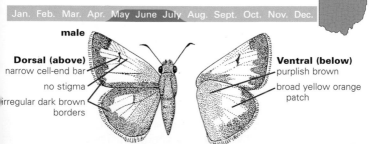

male

Dorsal (above)
narrow cell-end bar
no stigma
irregular dark brown
borders

Ventral (below)
purplish brown
broad yellow orange
patch

255

Ventral

Male | Female | Larva

Comments: A large skipper of wetland habitats with sedge, this lovely tawny-orange species has a distinctive but often faint pale ray through the ventral hindwing. Throughout much of its irregular eastern range, the Dion Skipper is quite localized in occurrence and seldom overly numerous. Nonetheless, it can be reliably encountered in most suitable habitat areas. Adults are sluggish fliers through wetland vegetation but can move very quickly if disturbed. Males readily perch on the tops of sedges or grasses but tend to be wary and difficult to closely approach. They do not wander far from their wetland haunts. Larvae overwinter.

Dion Skipper
Euphyes dion

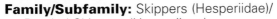

Family/Subfamily: Skippers (Hesperiidae)/
Banded Skippers (Hesperiinae)

Wingspan: 1.4–1.7" (3.6–4.3 cm)

Above: forewing is orange with broad, dark brown borders and a prominent black forewing stigma; hindwing is faint orange with a dark brown border and distinctly brighter elongated orange spot

Below: hindwing is tawny orange with faint light ray through the center

Sexes: dissimilar; female is primarily dark brown dorsally with yellow orange forewing spots and prominent single elongated orange hindwing spot

Egg: light green, laid singly on host leaves

Larva: blue-green with darker green dorsal line; white head marked with a black forehead spot bordered by orange brown vertical lines

Larval Host Plants: various sedges including Hairy Sedge

Habitat: wet meadows, marshes, drainage ditches, fens and bogs

Broods: single generation

Abundance: uncommon to occasional

Compare: Duke's Skipper (pg. 261) lacks bright orange scaling above, has rounder wings and prefers shadier habitats.

Resident

Jan. Feb. Mar. Apr. May June July Aug. Sept. Oct. Nov. Dec.

male

Dorsal (above)
prominent stigma
broad, dark borders
elongated orange spot

Ventral (below)
pale ray
tawny orange to reddish brown

257

Ventral

Larva

Comments: This is the smallest and most abundant "lesser fritillary" in Ohio. As its name suggests, the Meadow Fritillary inhabits a wide variety of open, moist landscapes from stream margins to alkaline fens and is quite tolerant of disturbed sites. Because of this broad habitat flexibility, the species has not mirrored the recent decline of the closely related Silver-bordered Fritillary. Adults have a rapid and somewhat erratic flight typically low to the ground just above the vegetation but frequently stop to nectar at available wildflowers.

Meadow Fritillary
Boloria bellona

Family/Subfamily: Brush-foots (Nymphalidae)/ Longwing Butterflies (Heliconiinae)

Wingspan: 1.25–1.90" (3.2–4.8 cm)

Above: orange with black bands and spots; elongated wings with squared-off forewing apex

Below: hindwing is mottled brown orange with violet frosting along the hindwing margin

Sexes: similar

Egg: tiny cream eggs laid singly and somewhat haphazardly near host

Larva: purplish black with fine yellow mottling and short cream-based brown spines

Larval Host Plants: violets

Habitat: old fields, wet meadows, pastures, roadside ditches, fens, moist prairies and stream corridors

Broods: two or more generations

Abundance: occasional to common

Compare: Silver-bordered Fritillary (pg. 273) has heavy black dorsal wing margins and metallic silver spot bands on the hindwing below.

Resident

Jan. Feb. Mar. Apr. May June July Aug. Sept. Oct. Nov. Dec.

Dorsal (above)
squared-off apex
basal half of wings darker

Ventral (below)
mottled brown orange
violet frosting along margin

Ventral

Male

Female

Larva

Comments: This is a reclusive skipper of forested swamps and other scrubby wetlands with sedges. A butterfly of contrasting color, it is a rich tawny-orange below compared to a much darker sooty black dorsal appearance. Primarily restricted to the northwest corner of the state, populations tend to be scattered and often highly localized. Adults maneuver low through sedges and other wetland vegetation with a slow, deliberate flight and can easily be overlooked.

Duke's Skipper
Euphyes dukesi

Family/Subfamily: Skippers (Hesperiidae)/
Banded Skippers (Hesperiinae)

Wingspan: 1.50–1.75" (3.8–4.4 cm)

Above: dark sooty brownish black with faint tawny
orange scaling along base of costal forewing margin;
wings are somewhat rounded

Below: rich brownish orange with black forewing base
and a pale ray through the hindwing

Sexes: similar, although female has small white forewing
spots

Egg: laid singly on the underside of host leaves

Larva: pale green; reddish brown head with a black spot
on the forehead surrounded by white

Larval Host Plants: various sedges including Hairy
Sedge

Habitat: wooded swamps and marshes

Broods: single generation

Abundance: rare to uncommon

Compare: Dion Skipper (pg. 257) has bright orange scaling above with more pointed forewings and prefers
more open, sunlit habitats.

Resident

Jan. Feb. Mar. Apr. May June July Aug. Sept. Oct. Nov. Dec.

male

Dorsal (above)
-unded sooty brown
wings

Ventral (below)
black toward base

pale ray

Male

Female   Male   Winter   Larva

Comments: Much debate centers on the origin of the butterfly's common name. One interpretation points to its narrow black forewing spot, which to many resembles a closed or partially closed eye. Others suggest that behavior is responsible. Individuals in the Deep South overwinter as adults in reproductive diapause. They are highly sedentary and seldom seen, but often become active on mild days to nectar at available flowers before disappearing again. It is an infrequent and uncommon vagrant or temporary colonist to Ohio. The adults produce distinct seasonal forms that vary dramatically in ventral hindwing coloration.

Sleepy Orange
Eurema nicippe

Family/Subfamily: Whites and Sulphurs (Pieridae)/ Sulphurs (Coliadinae)

Wingspan: 1.3–2.0" (3.3–5.1 cm)

Above: bright orange with broad irregular black wing borders; forewing cell bears small, elongated black spot

Below: hindwings seasonally variable; butter-yellow with brown markings in summer-form and tan to reddish brown with darker pattern elements in winter-form

Sexes: similar, although female is larger and less vibrant with heavier ventral hindwing pattern

Egg: white, laid singly on host leaves

Larva: green with thin, cream lateral stripe and numerous short hairs

Larval Host Plants: various wild and ornamental cassia species including Wild Senna and Maryland Senna

Habitat: open, disturbed sites including roadsides, vacant fields, agricultural land, parks and gardens

Broods: one or more generations

Abundance: rare to uncommon

Compare: Orange Sulphur (pg. 277) has a rounded black forewing cell spot, uniform black wing borders, and a distinct, red-rimmed silver spot on the ventral hindwing.

Visitor

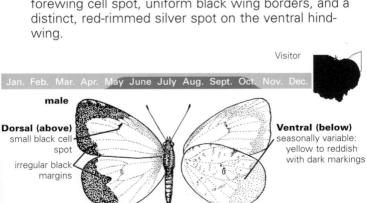

Jan. Feb. Mar. Apr. May June July Aug. Sept. Oct. Nov. Dec.

male

Dorsal (above)
small black cell spot

irregular black margins

Ventral (below)
seasonally variable: yellow to reddish with dark markings

263

Male

Larva

Comments: The range of Harris' Checkerspot within Ohio has been greatly reduced in recent years and the species may need state protection. It is closely associated with wetland habitats that support its sole larval host. As a result, populations tend to be rather small and highly localized but nevertheless can be fairly numerous when encountered. Adults have slow, gliding flight and maneuver close to the ground, periodically pausing to perch on low vegetation with their orange and black patterned wings outstretched. Both sexes occasionally seek nectar but are not prolific flower visitors. Males often gather at damp soil or animal dung.

Harris' Checkerspot
Chlosyne harrisii

Family/Subfamily: Brush-foots (Nymphalidae)/
True Brush-foots (Nymphalinae)

Wingspan: 1.4–2.0" (3.6–5.1 cm)

Above: tawny orange with black bands and broad black borders; often appearing extremely dark; hindwing has a row of white-centered, somewhat square black spots that typically touch the black border

Below: hindwing is reddish orange with three bands of white spots or crescents outlined in black

Sexes: similar, although female is somewhat larger

Egg: yellow, soon turning red, laid in clusters on the underside of host leaves

Larva: reddish orange with black transverse stripes and several rows of branched black spines; black head. Partially grown larvae overwinter and complete development the following spring.

Larval Host Plants: Flat-topped White Aster

Habitat: bogs, wet meadows, marshes and other wetlands

Broods: single generation

Abundance: rare to occasional; localized

Compare: Silvery Checkerspot (pg. 267) has incomplete row of silvery crescents on the ventral hindwing.

Resident

Jan. Feb. Mar. Apr. May June July Aug. Sept. Oct. Nov. Dec.

Dorsal (above)
primarily orange and black wings

black submarginal spots touching margin

Ventral (below)
white, orange and black checkered pattern

row of white crescents

Male

Ventral

Larva

Comments: This is a large checkerspot of moist forest clearings and adjacent open landscapes. The Silvery Checkerspot tends to fluctuate considerably in abundance from year to year, being locally common at times or nearly absent. In general, populations tend to be rather small and highly localized in close proximity to patches of available larval hosts. Adults have a relatively slow, gliding flight and maneuver close to the ground in open areas or along woodland roads. Males often gather at damp soil or animal dung. This species is rare north of Columbus.

Silvery Checkerspot
Chlosyne nycteis

Family/Subfamily: Brush-foots (Nymphalidae)/ True Brush-foots (Nymphalinae)

Wingspan: 1.4–2.0" (3.6–5.1 cm)

Above: tawny orange with black bands and wide black borders; hindwing has a submarginal row of white-centered, somewhat square black spots

Below: hindwing is pale yellow brown with a dark marginal patch and incomplete marginal row of silvery white crescents

Sexes: similar, although female is often much larger

Egg: cream, laid in large clusters on underside of leaves

Larva: dark brownish black; wide yellow orange lateral band and several rows of black spines; black head

Larval Host Plants: various Asteraceae family composites including Wing-stem, Gravelweed, White Crownbeard, asters, sunflowers, Cut-leaf Coneflower and Sneezeweed

Habitat: moist woodland openings, forest margins, stream corridors and adjacent wet meadows or semi-open areas

Broods: two generations

Abundance: uncommon to common

Compare: Harris' Checkerspot (pg. 265) has a complete submarginal row of silvery crescents on the hindwing below.

Resident

Jan. Feb. Mar. Apr. May June July Aug. Sept. Oct. Nov. Dec.

Dorsal (above)
submarginal row of white-centered black spots, not touching border

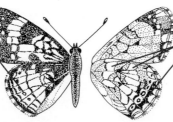

Ventral (below)
silvery bands

incomplete row of silvery white marginal crescents

Male

Male   Larva

Comments: This small butterfly has only recently been
considered a distinct species and there remains some
debate about its true taxonomic position. It is
extremely similar to the more widespread and abundant Pearl Crescent. In many instances, the two
species cannot be reliably separated in the field.
Although previously listed from Ohio, the earlier
records were based on incorrectly identified speci-
mens. As a result, the Northern Crescent should not
be considered part of Ohio's butterfly fauna.

Northern Crescent
Phyciodes selenis

Family/Subfamily: Brush-foots (Nymphalidae)/
True Brush-foots (Nymphalinae)

Wingspan: 1.5–1.9" (3.8–4.8 cm)

Above: tawny-orange with fine black bands, spots and
wing borders; male has large open areas of orange
that are typically clear without black veins; orange
antennal clubs

Below: hindwing is golden yellow brown with fine brown
markings and a dark marginal patch enclosing a pale
crescent

Sexes: similar, although female has more extensive dark
markings above

Egg: green, laid in clusters on the underside of host
leaves

Larva: dark brown with fine white mottling, a dark dorsal
line, a lateral cream stripe and numerous short, pinkish
gray branched spines

Larval Host Plants: various asters although exact
species are unknown

Habitat: moist open woodlands, forest edges, stream
margins and adjacent roadsides and fields

Broods: single generation

Abundance: rare

Compare: Pearl Crescent (pg. 249) has more
extensive black markings. Not present

Jan. Feb. Mar. Apr. May June July Aug. Sept. Oct. Nov. Dec.

Dorsal (above)
fine black markings

orange on
hindwing fairly
open

Ventral (below)
orange antennal clubs

dark marginal patch;
often without pale
crescent

269

Male

Larva

Comments: This is a large and distinctive skipper of semi-shaded, moist areas with abundant sedge. Like other wetland species, it has continued to lose habitat from expanding urban development and hydrologic alteration. As a result, populations tend to be widely scattered, highly localized and relatively low-density. Living up to its name, the Broad-winged Skipper has noticeably rounded, somewhat wide wings. Despite their size, adults maneuver through the wetland vegetation with a fairly slow, dancing flight and frequently alight on leaves. Both sexes may be encountered at the blossoms of nearby wetland flowers.

Broad-winged Skipper
Poanes viator

Family/Subfamily: Skippers (Hesperiidae)/ Banded Skippers (Hesperiinae)

Wingspan: 1.3–2.1" (3.3–5.3 cm)

Above: tawny orange with broad dark brown borders; forewing has rounded apex; hindwing has dark brown scaling along veins; male lacks stigma

Below: hindwing is tawny orange with distinct broad pale ray through pale spot band

Sexes: similar, although female has cream white spots on the forewing above

Egg: grayish, laid singly on the underside of host leaves

Larva: pale brown with an overall velvety appearance; reddish brown head

Larval Host Plants: various sedges and grasses including Annual Wild Rice, Common Reed, Hairy Sedge and Beaked Sedge

Habitat: forested swamps, wet meadows, fens, marshes, roadside ditches and associated clearings and margins

Broods: single generation

Abundance: rare to uncommon; localized

Compare: Dion Skipper (pg. 257) has more pointed forewings and has a less sharply contrasting broad yellow ray through the center of the hindwing below.

Resident

Jan. Feb. Mar. Apr. May June July Aug. Sept. Oct. Nov. Dec.

male

Dorsal (above)
squarish yellow orange spots
lacks stigma
broad dark borders

Ventral (below)
broad pale ray
pale spot band

271

Ventral

Larva

Comments: This small species is named for its distinctive metallic silver spot bands on the ventral hindwing that quickly distinguish it from the more abundant Meadow Fritillary with which it often flies. Restricted to open moist habitats, the Silver-bordered Fritillary has continued to decline within the state as a result of habitat loss or alteration. As a result, the species is currently listed as threatened in Ohio with only two small remaining metapopulations still present. Adults have a rapid and somewhat erratic flight typically low to the ground just above the vegetation.

Silver-bordered Fritillary
Boloria selene

Family/Subfamily: Brush-foots (Nymphalidae)/ Fritillaries (Heliconiinae)

Wingspan: 1.6–2.1" (4.1–5.3 cm)

Above: orange with black lines and spots; both wings have black borders that enclose small orange spots

Below: hindwing mottled orange and reddish brown with bands of iridescent silver spots

Sexes: similar

Egg: tiny cream eggs laid singly and somewhat haphazardly near host

Larva: dark gray with black patches, a orange-brown lateral stripe, numerous yellowish spines and two long, black prothoracic spines. Larvae overwinter.

Larval Host Plants: violets

Habitat: wet meadows, bogs, moist prairies, sedge marshes and adjacent fields and roadsides

Broods: three generations

Abundance: rare to occasional; localized

Compare: Meadow Fritillary (pg. 259) lacks the broad, black dorsal wing border and the silver spot bands on the hindwing below.

Resident

Jan. Feb. Mar. Apr. May June July Aug. Sept. Oct. Nov. Dec.

Dorsal (above)
ck, chain-like border with orange spots

Ventral (below)
distinctive metallic silver spot bands on hindwing

black submarginal spots

273

Ventral

Larva

Comments: The Variegated Fritillary is another southern
species that regularly wanders northward to colonize
much of Ohio each year. An intermediate of sorts
between true fritillaries and longwings, the butterfly's
spiny larvae are able to utilize both violets and passion
flowers as hosts. It has an affinity for just about any
open, sunny habitat and may occasionally be encountered in home gardens. Adults have a low, erratic flight
but regularly pause to nectar at available flowers.

Variegated Fritillary
Euptoieta claudia

Family/Subfamily: Brush-foots (Nymphalidae)/ Longwings (Heliconiinae)

Wingspan: 1.75–2.25" (4.4–5.7 cm)

Above: pale brownish orange with dark markings, narrow light median band and darker reddish orange base

Below: overall brown; forewing has basal orange scaling; hindwing mottled with tan, cream and dark brown; hindwing lacks silvery spots

Sexes: similar, although female is larger and has broader, more rounded wings

Egg: tiny cream eggs laid singly on host leaves and tendrils

Larva: reddish orange with black-spotted white stripes and black spines

Larval Host Plants: violets and passion flowers

Habitat: open, sunny sites including roadsides, pastures, old fields and utility easements

Broods: multiple generations

Abundance: rare to uncommon

Compare: Great Spangled Fritillary (pg. 297) and Aphrodite Fritillary (pg. 295) have large, conspicuous silvery spots on the ventral hindwing.

Visitor

Jan. Feb. Mar. Apr. May June July Aug. Sept. Oct. Nov. Dec.

male

Dorsal (above)
tawny orange with dark markings
darker wing bases
pale median band

Ventral (below)
orange base
mottled tan, cream and dark brown with no silver spots

Male   Female   Larva

Comments: This widespread North America species can be found in virtually any open landscape, but may be most abundant in commercial clover or alfalfa fields where it may occasionally become an economic pest. Because of this strong host preference, it is often called the Alfalfa Butterfly. It is a prolific colonizer and readily populates new areas where naturalized or native leguminous plants abound. Adults have a rapid, somewhat erratic flight and scurry close to the ground over low vegetation. Phenotypically variable, individuals produced in early spring or late fall are generally smaller and darker overall than warm-season adults.

Orange Sulphur
Colias eurytheme

Family/Subfamily: Whites and Sulphurs (Pieridae)/ Sulphurs (Coliadinae)

Wingspan: 1.6–2.4" (4.1–6.1 cm)

Above: bright yellow orange with black wing borders and black forewing cell spot; hindwing has central orange spot

Below: yellow with row of dark submarginal spots; hindwing has one or two central red-rimmed silvery spots

Sexes: similar, although female has yellow spots in broader black wing borders and are less vibrant; female is occasionally white

Egg: white, laid singly on host leaves

Larva: green with thin, cream lateral stripe and numerous short hairs

Larval Host Plants: Alfalfa, White Sweet Clover, White Clover and vetches

Habitat: open, sunny sites including roadsides, meadows, alfalfa or clover fields, parks, utility easements, vacant lots, pastures and home gardens

Broods: multiple generations

Abundance: occasional to abundant

Compare: Clouded Sulphur (pg. 327) lacks orange scaling above. White-form female Clouded and Orange may not be reliably distinguished in the field.

Resident

Jan. Feb. Mar. Apr. May June July Aug. Sept. Oct. Nov. Dec.

Dorsal (above)
black cell spot
smooth black borders
bright yellow orange
central orange spot

Ventral (below)
red-rimmed silvery spots
dark submarginal spots

Ventral

Larva

Comments: Unable to survive freezing temperatures, the Painted Lady typically overwinters in Mexico and annually colonizes much of the North American continent each summer. Its occurrence in Ohio, as well as many areas in the East, is somewhat sporadic with populations varying considerably in abundance from year to year. It can be found in just about any open, disturbed landscape where its weedy larval hosts abound. The adults have a rapid, erratic flight usually close to the ground but frequently stop to perch or nectar. The larvae construct individual shelters of loose webbing on the host.

Painted Lady
Vanessa cardui

Family/Subfamily: Brush-foots (Nymphalidae)/
True Brush-foots (Nymphalinae)

Wingspan: 1.75–2.40" (4.4–6.1 cm)

Above: pinkish orange with dark markings and small
white spots near tip of forewing

Below: brown with cream patches in ornate cobweb pattern; hindwing has row of four small eyespots and
marginal band of lavender spots

Sexes: similar

Egg: small pale green eggs laid singly on host leaves

Larva: variable; greenish yellow with black mottling to
charcoal with cream mottling and several rows of light-
colored, branched spines

Larval Host Plants: wide variety of plants in several
families including thistles and mallows; also Hollyhock

Habitat: open, disturbed sites including roadsides, old
fields, fallow agricultural land, pastures, utility easements and gardens

Broods: multiple generations

Abundance: uncommon to common

Compare: American Painted Lady (pg. 281) is overall
more orange, has a more extended forewing apex and
two large ventral hindwing eyespots.

Visitor

| Jan. | Feb. | Mar. | Apr. | May | June | July | Aug. | Sept. | Oct. | Nov. | Dec. |

male

Dorsal (above)
no small white spot
(as in American
Painted Lady)
connected black
markings

Ventral (below)
ornate cobweb patter
four submarginal
eyespots

279

Ventral

Larva

Comments: Considered a common, weedy butterfly, the American Painted Lady is often overlooked despite its attractiveness. The agate-like design on the underside of the wings is in sharp contrast to the bold orange and black pattern above. It may be encountered in just about any open, disturbed landscape. A nervous and wary butterfly, it is difficult to approach and closely observe. When disturbed, it takes off in a low, erratic flight but often returns to a nearby location just a few moments later. The larvae construct individual shelters on the host by spinning together leaves and flower heads with silk. They rest inside when not actively feeding.

American Painted Lady
Vanessa virginiensis

Family/Subfamily: Brush-foots (Nymphalidae)/
True Brush-foots (Nymphalinae)

Wingspan: 1.75–2.40" (4.4–6.1 cm)

Above: orange with dark marks and borders; forewing has
small white spots near extended and squared-off apex

Below: brown with ornate, cream cobweb pattern; hindwing has two large eyespots and narrow lavender
marginal band

Sexes: similar; females with broader wings

Egg: small pale green eggs laid singly on upper surface
of host leaves

Larva: variable; greenish yellow with narrow black bands
to black with cream bands and numerous red-based,
branched spines; pair of prominent white spots on
each segment; pupae occasionally overwinter

Larval Host Plants: various herbaceous composites
including cudweeds, Sweet Everlasting, pussy-toes
and others

Habitat: open, disturbed sites including roadsides, old
fields, pastures, utility easements and gardens

Broods: multiple generations

Abundance: occasional to common

Compare: Painted Lady (pg. 279) is pinker and has a row
of four small ventral hindwing eyespots.

Resident Visitor

Jan. Feb. Mar. Apr. May June July Aug. Sept. Oct. Nov. Dec.

Dorsal (above)
apex extended and
squared off

small white spot

disconnected black
markings

some blue in one or
more eyespots

Ventral (below)
small white spot

ornate cobweb pattern

two large eyespots

281

Summer

Ventral

Winter

Larva

Comments: The Eastern Comma, like its close relative
the Question Mark, survives the winter as an adult
hibernating in log piles, tree hollows or even within
manmade structures. Once warm weather returns in
spring, they become active and reproduce with the
resulting generation flying in early summer. A woodland
butterfly, it inhabits riparian forests, clearings and adjacent open, brushy areas. Adults have a rapid, erratic
flight and frequently perch on overhanging branches or
tree trunks. They are often quite wary and difficult to
closely approach. Both sexes seldom visit flowers, feeding instead at rotting fruit, dung, carrion and tree sap.

Eastern Comma
Polygonia comma

Family/Subfamily: Brush-foots (Nymphalidae)/
True Brush-foots (Nymphalinae)

Wingspan: 2.0–2.4" (5.1–6.1 cm)

Above: tawny orange with black borders and spots, irregular wing edge; forewing apex is extended and squared off; hindwing has single distinct tail; summer-form hindwing is primarily black; winter-form has increased orange

Below: seasonally variable; dead leaf appearance; summer-form is heavily mottled light and dark brown; winter-form is uniform brown with fine striations; hindwing has a single distinct curved silvery spot in center

Sexes: similar

Egg: green, laid singly or in small stacks on host leaves

Larva: variable; black to greenish brown with a white lateral band and several rows of white, branched spines

Larval Host Plants: Canadian Wood Nettle, American Elm, False Nettle, Common Hop and nettles

Habitat: deciduous forests, riparian woodlands, forest edges, parks, suburban yards and open brushy areas

Broods: two generations

Abundance: occasional to common

Compare: Question Mark (pg. 291) is larger and has silver spots shaped like a question mark in the center of the hindwing below.

Resident

Jan. Feb. Mar. Apr. May June July Aug. Sept. Oct. Nov. Dec.

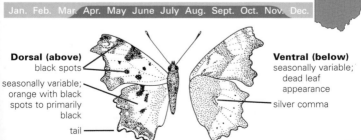

Dorsal (above)
black spots
seasonally variable; orange with black spots to primarily black
tail

Ventral (below)
seasonally variable; dead leaf appearance
silver comma

283

Ventral

Larva

Comments: This woodland butterfly is aptly named for its dull gray, highly striated wings below that closely resemble tree bark. Infrequent and somewhat reclusive, the Gray Comma occurs in small, highly localized colonies. It is most often encountered as a single, isolated individual along woodland trails, clearings or roadsides. Adults have an erratic, darting flight and frequently perch on tree trunks or on overhanging branches. They are often quite wary and difficult to closely approach. Both sexes seldom visit flowers, but prefer to feed at rotting fruit, dung, carrion and tree sap.

Gray Comma
Polygonia progne

Family/Subfamily: Brush-foots (Nymphalidae)/ True Brush-foots (Nymphalinae)

Wingspan: 2.1–2.4" (5.3–6.1 cm)

Above: tawny orange with heavy black borders and spots, highly irregular wing edge; forewing apex is extended and squared off; hindwing bears a single short, stubby tail; hindwing border encloses a row of small yellow orange spots

Below: dull gray with fine striations and a narrow silver comma in center of hindwing; darker toward base

Sexes: similar

Egg: green, laid singly on host leaves

Larva: variable; yellow brown with transverse black lines between segments, dark botches and dashes, and several rows of pale yellow and black branched spines

Larval Host Plants: gooseberries

Habitat: moist deciduous woodlands, clearings, woodland roads, forest edges, swamps and adjacent open, brushy areas

Broods: two generations

Abundance: rare to occasional; localized

Compare: Eastern Comma (pg. 283) is larger with less jagged wing margins; lacks dull gray ventral wing coloration.

Resident

Jan. Feb. Mar. Apr. May June July Aug. Sept. Oct. Nov. Dec.

Dorsal (above)
irregular wing edge

yellowish orange spots in dark border

Ventral (below)
fine gray brown striations

two-toned appearance

silver comma

Ventral

Larva

Comments: The Atlantis Fritillary is primarily a northland butterfly of boreal forest openings and adjacent fields and meadows. Its range dips southward and just enters the northeast corner of Ohio. A separate, disjunct population occurs in the higher mountains of bordering West Virginia. Despite its occurrence within the state, it is considered a rare find and is typically encountered as isolated individuals. Like other fritillaries, the adults have a swift and rapid flight but readily pause to feed at available flowers.

Atlantis Fritillary
Speyeria atlantis

Family/ Subfamily: Brush-foots (Nymphalidae)/ Longwings and Fritillaries (Heliconiinae)

Wingspan: 2.40–2.75" (6.1–7.0 cm)

Above: orange with black spots and broad, solid black borders

Below: hindwing is dark purplish brown with metallic silver spots and a narrow yellowish tan submarginal band

Sexes: similar, although female is typically larger and more golden orange

Egg: small cream eggs are laid singly and somewhat haphazardly on or near host

Larva: dark brown with fine yellowish striations, black blotches, a black dorsal stripe outlined in yellow and numerous orange-brown spines

Larval Host Plants: various violets

Habitat: open woodlands, forest clearings and margins, wetlands, pastures, old fields and roadsides

Abundance: rare

Broods: single generation

Compare: Aphrodite Fritillary (pg. 295) lacks the solid black dorsal wing borders and the dark purplish brown ventral hindwing.

Stray

Jan. Feb. Mar. Apr. May June July Aug. Sept. Oct. Nov. Dec.

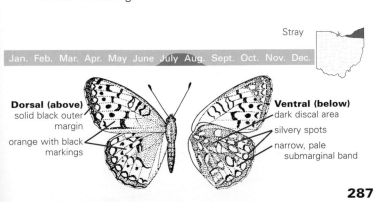

Dorsal (above)
solid black outer margin

orange with black markings

Ventral (below)
dark discal area

silvery spots

narrow, pale submarginal band

Male

Ventral   Winter   Larva

Comments: This southern resident is a rare vagrant to
Ohio. Its name comes from one of its primary larval
hosts. Although brilliant reddish orange dorsally, the
leaf-like pattern of its wings below provides superb
camouflage. It produces distinct seasonal forms that
vary in wing shape and to a lesser extent in ground
color. Individuals produced late in the season survive the
winter in reproductive diapause. Adults have a strong,
darting flight and perch with wings closed on tree
trunks, branches or on the ground. They can be quite a
challenge to find, let alone closely approach. It does not
nectar at flowers but prefers rotting fruit and sap.

Goatweed Butterfly
Anaea andria

Family/Subfamily: Brush-foots (Nymphalidae)/ Leafwings (Charaxinae)

Wingspan: 2.25–3.00" (5.7–7.6 cm)

Above: pointed forewings and hindwing tail; male is bright reddish orange; female is lighter orange with dark markings and pale band along wing margins

Below: seasonally variable; brownish gray resembling a dead leaf; winter-form is more heavily patterned, has longer hindwing tails and a more pronounced hooked forewing apex

Sexes: similar, although female is lighter with more extensive dorsal markings

Egg: gray-green, laid singly on host leaves

Larva: gray-green with light head and numerous tiny light spots

Larval Host Plants: Goatweed and Silver Croton

Habitat: dry pinelands, woodland edges and adjacent open areas

Broods: one or more generations where resident

Abundance: rare

Compare: Question Mark (pg. 291) has irregular wing edges, an extended and squared-off forewing apex and black dorsal forewing spots.

Stray

Jan. Feb. Mar. Apr. May June July Aug. Sept. Oct. Nov. Dec.

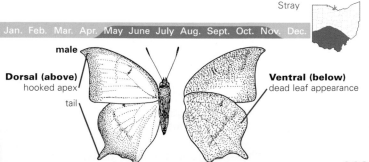

male

Dorsal (above)
hooked apex

tail

Ventral (below)
dead leaf appearance

Summer

Ventral

Winter

Larva

Comments: This large anglewing gets its name from the small silvery hindwing marks that resembles (with some imagination) a rudimentary question mark. In sharp contrast to its bright orange dorsal surface, the wings below are cryptically mottled with brown to help the butterfly resemble a dead leaf when at rest. Found primarily in woodlands, adults have a strong, rapid flight but frequently alight on overhanging branches, tree trunks or leaf litter. Wary and nervous, they are often difficult to closely approach. Males are inquisitive and aggressively investigate virtually any passing insects. Both sexes visit rotting fruit, dung, carrion and sap.

Question Mark
Polygonia interrogationis

Family/Subfamily: Brush-foots (Nymphalidae)/
True Brush-foots (Nymphalinae)

Wingspan: 2.25–3.00" (5.7–7.6 cm)

Above: orange with black spots, narrow lavender borders and irregular, jagged edges; seasonally variable; summer-form hindwing is primarily black; winter-form has increased orange on hindwing

Below: seasonally variable; pinkish brown dead leaf appearance; hindwing has two, small median silvery spots that form a question mark

Sexes: similar

Egg: green, laid singly or in small groups on top of each other on host leaves

Larva: gray to black with orange and cream stripes and spots and several rows of branched spines

Larval Host Plants: Sugarberry, American Elm, Winged Elm, also False Nettle and Stinging Nettle

Habitat: deciduous forests, moist woodlands, forest edges and adjacent open areas

Broods: two generations

Abundance: occasional to common

Compare: Eastern Comma (pg. 283) is smaller and has a comma-shaped silver spot in the center of the hindwing below.

Resident

Jan. Feb. Mar. Apr. May June July Aug. Sept. Oct. Nov. Dec.

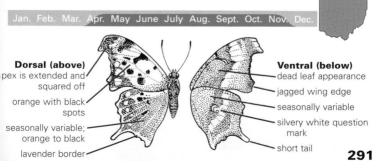

Dorsal (above)
apex is extended and squared off

orange with black spots

seasonally variable; orange to black

lavender border

Ventral (below)
dead leaf appearance

jagged wing edge

seasonally variable

silvery white question mark

short tail

291

Male

Ventral

Larva

Comments: The colorful Viceroy is usually found in or near wetland areas in close proximity to its larval hosts. Males perch on overhanging branches and occasionally dart out to investigate passing objects or to take periodic exploratory flights. Both sexes tend to be somewhat wary and difficult to closely approach. Although once thought to be a palatable mimic of the distasteful Monarch, studies have shown that both species are actually distasteful to certain predators. Adults are often encountered at a variety of flowers but will also feed at dung, carrion, fermenting fruit and tree sap.

Viceroy
Limenitis archippus

Family/Subfamily: Brush-foots (Nymphalidae)/ Admirals and Relatives (Limenitidinae)

Wingspan: 2.6–3.2" (6.6–8.1 cm)

Above: orange with black markings, veins and broad wing borders; borders contain central row of small, white spots; forewing has black postmedian band and white spots; hindwing has distinct thin, black post-median line

Below: as above with lighter orange coloration and increased white markings

Sexes: similar

Egg: gray-green, laid singly on tip of host leaves

Larva: mottled green, brown and cream with two long, knobby horns on thorax

Larval Host Plants: various willows including Black Willow, Carolina Willow and Weeping Willow; also Cottonwood

Habitat: pond edges, wetlands, roadside ditches and moist areas supporting willows

Broods: two generations

Abundance: occasional to common; localized

Compare: Monarch (pg. 301) is larger and lacks black postmedian hindwing line.

Resident

Jan. Feb. Mar. Apr. May June July Aug. Sept. Oct. Nov. Dec.

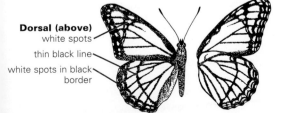

Dorsal (above)
white spots
thin black line
white spots in black border

Ventral (below)
orange with black bands containing white spots

293

Ventral

Larva

Comments: This widespread northern species displays a much stronger dependence on prairie habitats than its more abundant relative the Great Spangled Fritillary with which it is easily confused. As a result, the Aphrodite Fritillary tends occur in smaller, more highly localized populations across Ohio but may still be relatively common when encountered. Individuals are also less likely to wander far from suitable habitat areas. Adults have a swift, directed flight and are best observed at flowers. A patrolling species, males actively search for females, often following long, circular routes.

Aphrodite Fritillary
Speyeria aphrodite

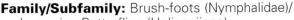

Family/Subfamily: Brush-foots (Nymphalidae)/ Longwing Butterflies (Heliconiinae)

Wingspan: 2.7–3.3" (6.9–8.4 cm)

Above: bright orange with heavy black lines and spots

Below: variable; hindwing is dark orange brown to reddish brown with numerous large metallic silver spots and a narrow yellowish submarginal band

Sexes: similar, although female is larger with darker brown wing bases, more pronounced black markings and paler golden orange wings

Egg: tiny cream eggs laid singly and somewhat haphazardly near host leaves

Larva: velvety black with several rows of black spines; lateral two rows of spines reddish brown with black tips

Larval Host Plants: various violets

Habitat: open woodlands, old fields, moist meadows, prairies, pastures, forest edges and roadsides

Broods: single generation

Abundance: rare to occasional, locally common

Compare: Great Spangled Fritillary (pg. 297) is slightly larger and has wide yellowish submarginal band on the hindwing below.

Resident

Jan. Feb. Mar. Apr. May June July Aug. Sept. Oct. Nov. Dec.

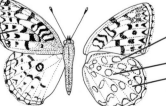

Dorsal (above)
bright orange with heavy black lines and spots

Ventral (below)
large metallic silver spots

reddish brown base

narrow yellowish submarginal band

Female
Female   Larva

Comments: Easily the most conspicuous and wide-spread fritillary in Ohio, the Great Spangled Fritillary is not nearly as localized and habitat-restricted as other members of the genus. Adults have a strong, directed flight but frequently pause to nectar, being particularly fond of milkweed, Bee-balm and thistles. It is not unusual to see several individuals clustering on a single flower. Males typically emerge several weeks before females. Although females may be on the wing as early as the beginning of July, they do not begin laying eggs until late summer and often fly well into September. Newly hatched larvae overwinter.

Great Spangled Fritillary
Speyeria cybele

Family/Subfamily: Brush-foots (Nymphalidae)/
Longwing Butterflies (Heliconiinae)

Wingspan: 2.9–3.8" (7.1–9.7 cm)

Above: bright orange with heavy black lines and spots

Below: variable; hindwing is dark orange brown to brown
with numerous large metallic silver spots and a broad
yellowish submarginal band

Sexes: similar, although female is larger with darker
brown wing bases, more pronounced black markings
and paler golden orange to pale yellowish wings

Egg: tiny cream eggs laid singly and somewhat haphazardly on or host leaves

Larva: velvety black with several rows of reddish orange-
based black spines

Larval Host Plants: various violets

Habitat: open deciduous woodlands, forest margins,
roadsides, pastures, old fields, wet meadows, prairies
and utility easements

Broods: single generation

Abundance: occasional to abundant

Compare: Aphrodite Fritillary (pg. 295) is smaller, less
common and has a narrow yellowish submarginal band
on the ventral hindwing.

Resident

Jan. Feb. Mar. Apr. May June July Aug. Sept. Oct. Nov. Dec.

Dorsal (above)
heavy black lines and
spots
darker base

Ventral (below)
large metallic silver
spots
wide submarginal
yellowish band

297

Female

Ventral

Larva

Comments: The beautiful Regal Fritillary has disappeared from much of its previous eastern range as a result of expanding agriculture, urban development and lack of proper habitat management. Once widespread and abundant across much of Ohio, it is currently listed as endangered by the Ohio DNR and has not been recorded from the state since 1991. It now serves as a charismatic icon for prairie conservation. Adults have a fast, steady flight and maneuver low over open fields. Individuals often wander extensively and may be encountered far from their population of origin. It is exceedingly fond of flowers.

Regal Fritillary
Speyeria idalia

Family/Subfamily: Brush-foots (Nymphalidae)/ Longwing Butterflies (Heliconiinae)

Wingspan: 3.1–4.0" (7.9–10.2 cm)

Above: forewing is bright reddish orange with black markings; hindwing is black with a bluish cast; male has an outer row of orange spots and a inner row of white spots on hindwing

Below: hindwing is dark brown with numerous black-edged white (not silvery) spots

Sexes: similar, although female is larger with both rows of hindwing spots white

Egg: tiny cream eggs laid singly and somewhat haphazardly near host leaves

Larva: gray black; ochre yellow to reddish orange dorsal band and similar colored lateral mottling; dorsal spines are silvery white with black tips while those along the sides have orange bases

Larval Host Plants: Bird's-foot Violet

Habitat: tallgrass prairie, wet meadows, marshes and adjacent fields, roadsides and pastures

Broods: single generation

Abundance: rare; localized

Compare: unique

Resident

| Jan. | Feb. | Mar. | Apr. | May | June | July | Aug. | Sept. | Oct. | Nov. | Dec. |

male

Dorsal (above)
reddish orange

black with a bluish cast

white postmedian spots

orange submarginal spots

Ventral (below)
dark brown hindwing

black-edged white spots

299

Female

Ventral   Larva

Comments: The Monarch is undoubtedly the most familiar and widely recognized butterfly in North America. Its annual fall mass migration is one of the greatest natural events undertaken by any organism on Earth. Adults have a strong, soaring flight and are abundant garden visitors. The striped larvae feed on plants in the Milkweed family from which they sequester toxic chemicals that render them and the resulting adults distasteful to certain predators. The adult butterflies advertise this unpalatability in dramatic fashion with their bold orange and black coloration.

Monarch
Danaus plexippus

Family/Subfamily: Brush-foots (Nymphalidae)/ Milkweed Butterflies (Danainae)

Wingspan: 3.5–4.0" (8.9–10.2 cm)

Above: orange with black veins and wing borders; black borders have two rows of small white spots; male has small black androconial scent patch on center of hind-wing

Below: as above with lighter orange coloration

Sexes: similar; female lacks black scent patch

Egg: white, laid singly on host leaves

Larva: white with transverse black and yellow stripes; there is a pair of long, black filaments on each end

Larval Host Plants: various milkweeds including Swamp Milkweed and Common Milkweed

Habitat: open, sunny locations including old fields, road-sides, utility easements, meadows, prairies, agricultural land, parks and gardens

Broods: multiple generations

Abundance: occasional to common

Compare: Viceroy (pg. 293) is smaller and has a black postmedian line through the hindwing.

Visitor

Jan. Feb. Mar. Apr. May June July Aug. Sept. Oct. Nov. Dec.

male

Dorsal (above)
white spots
bright orange
two rows of white spots
black veins
scent patch on males only

Ventral (below)
lighter yellow orange

301

Male

Female pg. 63   Male   Larva

Comments: The Diana Fritillary is primarily restricted to the moist, deciduous forests throughout the Appalachian Mountains from West Virginia to Mississippi. Although historically found within the state, urban development and related human land use practices have eliminated much of its previously available habitat, resulting in extirpation of the species.

Diana Fritillary
Speyeria diana

Family/Subfamily: Brush-foots (Nymphalidae)/ Longwing Butterflies (Heliconiinae)

Wingspan: 3.5–4.4" (8.9–11.2 cm)

Above: male is dark unmarked blackish brown with bright orange on the outer third; female is black basally with white and iridescent blue spots on outer half

Below: forewing is orange with heavy black markings toward base; male hindwing is brownish orange with two rows of small narrow silver dashes; female hindwing is chocolate brown

Sexes: dissimilar; female is black basally with white and iridescent blue spots on outer half; ventral hindwing is chocolate brown

Egg: tiny cream eggs laid singly and somewhat haphazardly near host leaves

Larva: velvety black with several rows of reddish orange based black spines

Larval Host Plants: various woodland violets

Habitat: rich, moist deciduous mountain woodlands, stream corridors, forested roads, clearings and adjacent open areas

Broods: single generation

Abundance: extirpated

Compare: unique

No longer present

Jan. Feb. Mar. Apr. May June July Aug. Sept. Oct. Nov. Dec.

male

Dorsal (above)
black
orange
female primarily black
and blue)

Ventral (below)
black markings toward base

lacks prominent silvery hindwing spots characteristic of other fritillaries

303

Ventral   Larva

Comments: The Common Checkered-Skipper is quickly recognized by its black and white checkerboard pattern. Widespread and generally common across much of the central and southern U.S., the species expands its range to temporarily colonize many northern locations each year and is a regular seasonal visitor to Ohio, where it tends to be most frequently encountered in late summer and early fall. The small adults scurry low over weedy vegetation with a fast, erratic flight. The nervous and aggressive males seem to continuously engage one another in a frenzy of activity.

Common Checkered-Skipper
Pyrgus communis

Family/Subfamily: Skippers (Hesperiidae)/ Spread-wing Skippers (Pyrginae)

Wingspan: 0.75–1.25" (1.9–3.2 cm)

Above: male is black with numerous small, white spots and some bluish white scaling on base of wings and thorax; female is dark brown with reduced white scaling

Below: white with tan to brown irregular bands and spots

Sexes: similar, although female has reduced white markings

Egg: pale green, laid singly on host leaves

Larva: gray-green with dark dorsal stripe, light side stripes and black head

Larval Host Plants: various mallow family plants including Common Mallow

Habitat: open, disturbed sites including roadsides, old fields, utility easements and fallow agricultural land

Broods: multiple generations

Abundance: rare to occasional; localized

Compare: Grizzled Skipper (pg. 43) appears darker with fewer white spots on the wings above, and is primarily associated with open oak woodlands in the southeastern corner of the state.

Visitor

Jan. Feb. Mar. Apr. May June July Aug. Sept. Oct. Nov. Dec.

Dorsal (above)
fringe checkered to apex

generally black and white above

marginal spots much smaller than those in submarginal row

Ventral (below)
distinct bands

paler below

305

Dorsal

Larva

Comments: The West Virginia White is a small, ghostly white butterfly of early spring. Unlike most other members of the family, it is primarily restricted to rich deciduous woodlands. It is a poor pioneer species, reluctant to cross large expanses of open habitat to colonize nearby patches of available woodland or second growth forest. Its meandering eastern range brings it into the northwest corner of Ohio where it may at times be locally abundant. Adults have a low, weak flight and maneuver slowly along the forest floor, stopping occasionally to nectar. Males frequently puddle at damp ground along woodland trails or roads.

West Virginia White
Pieris virginiensis

Family/Subfamily: Whites and Sulphurs (Pieridae)/ Whites (Pierinae)

Wingspan: 1.2–1.6" (3.0–4.1 cm)

Above: unmarked white to smoky white with black scaling along costal margin and wing bases

Below: hindwings white with brown gray scaling along veins

Sexes: similar, although female typically appears more smoky gray on the wings above

Egg: greenish white, laid singly on underside of leaves

Larva: gray green with longitudinal yellow orange stripes and covered with small black dots

Larval Host Plants: toothworts and rockcress

Habitat: rich, moist deciduous woodlands, forest edges and occasionally adjacent meadows or open areas

Broods: single generation

Abundance: rare to occasional; often quite localized in occurrence

Compare: The Cabbage White (pg. 315) has charcoal wingtips, one or two postmedian black spots on the dorsal forewing and lacks brown-gray scaling along the veins on the ventral hindwing.

Resident

Jan. Feb. Mar. Apr. May June July Aug. Sept. Oct. Nov. Dec.

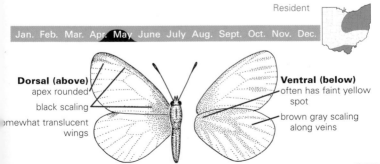

Dorsal (above)
apex rounded
black scaling
somewhat translucent wings

Ventral (below)
often has faint yellow spot
brown gray scaling along veins

307

Ventral

Larva

Comments: This delicate species is one of the earliest
spring butterflies. The Olympia Marble is now considered extirpated from Ohio. It historically occurred in
open oak barrens in the extreme southeastern portion
of the state. Adults maneuver close to the ground with
a direct, rapid flight. Males actively patrol for females
and often frequent the tops of exposed, dry ridges.
Freshly emerged individuals typically have a pinkish or
rosy flush on the ventral hindwing, which fades with
age.

Olympia Marble
Euchloe olympia

Family/Subfamily: Whites and Sulphurs (Pieridae)/ Whites (Pierinae)

Wingspan: 1.25–1.75" (3.2–4.4 cm)

Above: white with black scaling at bases; forewing has charcoal apex and black cell-end bar; hindwing often has faint black scaling at vein endings

Below: hindwing is white with yellow-green marbling; fresh individuals have a pinkish flush near the base of the hindwing

Sexes: similar

Egg: white, laid singly on host leaves or flower buds

Larva: gray with a yellow stripe, a yellow-white lateral stripe and numerous black dots

Larval Host Plants: rockcress

Habitat: dry ridges in semi-open oak woodlands

Broods: single generation

Abundance: extirpated

Compare: Falcate Orangetip (pg. 311) has hooked wingtips and extensive gray-green marbling on the hindwing below; males have orange forewing apex.

No longer present

| Jan. | Feb. | Mar. | Apr. | May | June | July | Aug. | Sept. | Oct. | Nov. | Dec. |

Dorsal (above)
gray apex

black bar at end of cell

wings somewhat translucent

Ventral (below)
restricted yellow green marbling

309

Male

Ventral | Female | Larva

Comments: This small, delicate butterfly provides a wel-
come hint of approaching spring by appearing during
the cool, unpredictable early spring. Aptly named, it
can be quickly identified by its distinctive hooked or
falcate wingtips. Although considered a forest species,
it avoids dense shade and is typically found in open,
thinly wooded areas and adjacent clearings. Adults
have a quick, erratic flight and maneuver adeptly close
to the ground through forest vegetation. Both sexes
visit a variety of early spring flowers and readily nectar
on the blossoms of their larval hosts. Males actively
patrol hilltops and other open areas for females.

Falcate Orangetip
Anthocharis midea

Family/Subfamily: Whites and Sulphurs (Pieridae)/ Whites (Pierinae)

Wingspan: 1.25–1.75" (3.2–4.4 cm)

Above: white; forewing has a small black cell spot and distinctive hooked (falcate) tip; male has orange tips on forewings; female has white forewing tips

Below: hindwings white; heavily marbled with gray

Sexes: dissimilar; male has orange forewing tips

Egg: orange, laid singly on leaves, stems or flower buds

Larva: blue-green with a narrow yellow orange dorsal stripe, bright white lateral stripe and small black dots

Larval Host Plants: herbaceous plants in mustard family including rockcress, Field Peppergrass, Cut-leaf Toothwort, bittercress, Shepherd's Purse and Garlic Mustard

Habitat: lowland forest clearings, riparian woodlands, open deciduous forests and associated margins and clearings, hilltops and occasionally roadsides

Broods: single generation

Abundance: uncommon to common, often localized

Compare: Olympia Marble (pg. 309) lacks the falcate wingtips and orange apex in males; has sparse yellow-green ventral hindwing marbling in distinct broad bands.

Resident

Jan. Feb. Mar. Apr. May June July Aug. Sept. Oct. Nov. Dec.

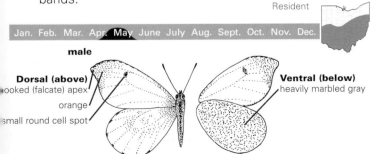

male

Dorsal (above)
hooked (falcate) apex
orange
small round cell spot

Ventral (below)
heavily marbled gray

311

Male

Female

Larva

Comments: The Checkered White is likely only a regular temporary seasonal colonist in Ohio, although wide-ranging throughout much of the East. As a result, populations often fluctuate from year to year and tend to be most numerous late in the season. Adults have a quick, erratic flight and can often be a challenge to closely approach. The sexes differ dramatically in the amount of dark scaling on the wings and can generally be told apart even from a distance. Individuals produced in early spring or late fall (under cooler conditions and shorter daylengths) are typically smaller, darker and more heavily patterned.

Checkered White
Pontia protodice

Family/Subfamily: Whites and Sulphurs (Pieridae)/ Whites (Pierinae)

Wingspan: 1.25–2.00" (3.2–5.1 cm)

Above: male is white with charcoal markings on forewing and immaculate hindwing; female is grayish white with extensive black or grayish brown checkered markings on both wings

Below: hindwings white with grayish markings and yellow-green scaling along the veins; seasonally variable; cool season individuals are more heavily patterned

Sexes: similar, although female has more black markings

Egg: yellow, laid singly on host leaves or flowers

Larva: gray; longitudinal yellow-orange stripe, black dots

Larval Host Plants: Virginia Peppergrass, Common Pepperweed, Garden Yellowrocket, Shepherd's Purse

Habitat: open, disturbed sites including roadsides, pastures, utility easements, railroad rights-of-way, vacant fields and fallow agricultural land

Broods: multiple generations

Abundance: rare to occasional

Compare: Cabbage White (pg. 315) has charcoal wingtips and distinctive single or double dorsal forewing spots. West Virginia White (pg. 307) lacks the gray checkered pattern and is primarily restricted to deciduous woodlands.

Visitor

Jan. Feb. Mar. Apr. May June July Aug. Sept. Oct. Nov. Dec.

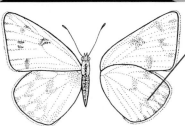

male

Dorsal (above)
white with black checkered pattern

Ventral (below)
seasonally variable; cool season forms are more heavily patterned

Male

Larva

Comments: Accidentally introduced from Europe around 1860, the Cabbage White (or European Cabbage Butterfly) quickly radiated across much of North America. It is generally abundant throughout Ohio. Readily encountered in almost any open, disturbed area, it may be particularly noticeable in home vegetable gardens or farmers' fields where it utilizes a variety of cultivated larval hosts. As a result, it is one of the few butterfly species considered to be a serious agricultural and garden pest. Adults have a slow, somewhat awkward flight and are easy to observe. The wings beneath are delicately shaded with yellow.

Cabbage White
Pieris rapae

Family/Subfamily: Whites and Sulphurs (Pieridae)/ Whites (Pierinae)

Wingspan: 1.5–2.0" (3.8–5.1 cm)

Above: male is white with single black postmedian forewing spot and wing tips; female is white with two black postmedian forewing spots

Below: forewing white with two black spots and yellow tips; hindwing immaculate whitish yellow

Sexes: similar, although female has two black spots on forewing

Egg: white, laid singly on host leaves and flowers

Larva: green with small lateral yellow dashes and numerous short hairs

Larval Host Plants: cultivated and wild members of the Mustard Family including Virginia Peppergrass, Wild Mustard, Wild Radish, broccoli, cabbage, turnip, cauliflower and radish

Habitat: open, disturbed sites including vacant lots, roadsides, old fields, utility easements, agricultural land and gardens; occasionally open woodland

Broods: multiple generations

Abundance: occasional to abundant

Compare: Checkered White (pg. 313) has more extensive checkered black markings and is typically less abundant.

Resident

Jan. Feb. Mar. Apr. May June July Aug. Sept. Oct. Nov. Dec.

female

Dorsal (above)
black apex

one (male) or two (female) black spots

black spot

Ventral (below)
yellowish apex

yellowish hindwing

White-form female

Male pg. 327

Larva

Comments: Like its close relative the Orange Sulphur
with which it is often flies, this aggressive colonizer
has likely benefitted from the spread of agriculture and
human land use practices. Although it may be encountered in just about any open habitat, it is generally
most abundant in commercial clover or alfalfa fields
where it may occasionally become a pest. It is sexually
dimorphic and seasonally variable. Both yellow and
white-form females are common and adults produced
under cool, early spring or late fall conditions tend to
be smaller and darker below than those of the summer generations. Adults have a quick, erratic flight.

Clouded Sulphur
Colias philodice

Family/Subfamily: Whites and Sulphurs (Pieridae)/ Sulphurs (Coliadinae)

Wingspan: 1.90–2.75" (4.8–7.0 cm)

Above: clear lemon yellow with bold, solid black wing borders and a prominent black forewing cell spot; hindwing has a central orange spot

Below: yellow to greenish yellow; row (often faint or occasionally absent) of dark submarginal spots; pink wing fringes; hindwing has central red-rimmed silvery spot and adjacent smaller satellite spot

Sexes: dissimilar; female is less vibrant, often has more black scaling and broader black borders enclosing yellow spots; also has a common white form

Egg: white, laid singly on host leaves

Larva: blue-green with a lateral cream stripe marked in black below and often containing faint red dashes

Larval Host Plants: Alfalfa, Red Clover, White Clover and White Sweet Clover

Habitat: open, sunny sites including roadsides, meadows, alfalfa fields, parks, pastures and home gardens

Broods: multiple generations

Abundance: rare to occasional

Compare: White-form female of Orange Sulphur (pg. 277) may not be reliably distinguished in the field.

Resident

| Jan. | Feb. | Mar. | Apr. | May | June | July | Aug. | Sept. | Oct. | Nov. | Dec. |

male

Dorsal (above)
black spot
yellow with no orange scaling
smooth black border
orange spot

Ventral (below)
two silvery spots
pink fringe
black dusting on hindwing
partial postmedian row of dark spots

317

Ventral   Larva

Comments: Easily our most elegant species, the long-tailed black-and-white-striped Zebra Swallowtail can be confused with no other resident butterfly. Adults have a low, rapid flight and adeptly maneuver through the understory or among shrubby vegetation. Seldom found far from stands of its larval host, it is unlikely to be encountered in highly developed areas although may occasionally wander into nearby home gardens in search of nectar. The swallowtail has a proportionately short proboscis and is thus unable to feed at many long, tubular flowers. It instead prefers composites, and is regularly attracted to white flowers.

Zebra Swallowtail
Eurytides marcellus

Family/Subfamily: Swallowtails (Papilionidae)/ Swallowtails (Papilioninae)

Wingspan: 2.5–4.0" (6.4–10.2 cm)

Above: white with black stripes and long, slender tails; hindwings bear a bright red patch above the eyespot; spring-forms are smaller, lighter and have shorter tails

Below: as above, but with a red stripe through hindwing

Sexes: similar

Egg: light green, laid singly on host leaves or budding branches

Larva: several color forms; may be green, green with light blue and yellow stripes or charcoal with white and yellow stripes

Larval Host Plants: pawpaw

Habitat: open deciduous woodlands, stream corridors, old fields, forest edges and roads

Broods: multiple generations

Abundance: occasional to common

Compare: unique

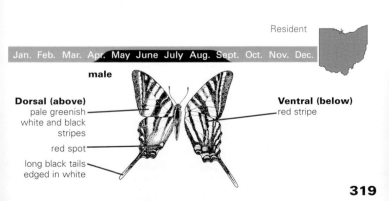

Resident

Jan. Feb. Mar. Apr. May June July Aug. Sept. Oct. Nov. Dec.

male

Dorsal (above)
pale greenish white and black stripes

red spot

long black tails edged in white

Ventral (below)
red stripe

Male

Larva

Comments: As its name implies, the Dainty Sulphur is
our smallest sulphur. Although common and widespread throughout much of the Deep South, it is a rare
vagrant or temporary seasonal colonist to Ohio and
should be considered a "good find" when encountered. The majority of all state records are from late
summer and fall. Adults have a low, erratic flight and
may be easily overlooked. The butterfly produces distinct seasonal forms that vary considerably in ventral
hindwing coloration. Individuals produced under cool
temperatures and short daylengths have increased
green scaling.

Dainty Sulphur
Nathalis iole

Family/Subfamily: Whites and Sulphurs (Pieridae)/ Sulphurs (Coliadinae)

Wingspan: 0.75–1.25" (1.9–3.2 cm)

Above: lemon yellow with black forewing tip and black bar along trailing edge of forewing; female has orange-yellow hindwings with more extensive black markings

Below: hindwings yellow with greenish markings; seasonally variable; winter-form more heavily pigmented

Sexes: similar, although black markings more extensive on female

Egg: yellow, laid singly on host leaves

Larva: green with thin, lateral yellow and lavender stripes

Larval Host Plants: Spanish Needles, Green Carpetweed and Sneezeweed

Habitat: dry and open disturbed sites including roadsides, pastures, utility easements, vacant fields and fallow agricultural land

Broods: multiple generations

Abundance: rare

Compare: Little Sulphur (pg. 323) is larger, has rounder wings, lacks the orange scaling along the costal margin of the ventral forewing and lacks the green scaling on the ventral hindwing.

Stray

Jan. Feb. Mar. Apr. May June July Aug. Sept. Oct. Nov. Dec.

male

Dorsal (above)
black apex
diffuse black bar

Ventral (below)
black spots
orange scaling
seasonally variable;
yellow olive to
heavily dusted
with black

321

Male

Female Male Larva

Comments: The Little Sulphur is a small yellow butterfly
with a low, scurrying flight and an affinity for dry, open
habitats. A year-round resident of the Deep South and
a highly effective colonizer, it readily moves northward
with the onset of warm temperatures to establish
temporary breeding populations throughout much of
the eastern U.S. It is a frequent but sporadic vagrant
or seasonal colonist to Ohio, and may be particularly
common in late summer and early fall. Like other
members of the genus, it produces different seasonal
forms that vary in coloration, behavior and reproductive
activity.

Little Sulphur
Eurema lisa

Family/Subfamily: Whites and Sulphurs (Pieridae)/ Sulphurs (Coliadinae)

Wingspan: 1.0–1.6" (2.5–4.1 cm)

Above: bright yellow with black forewing tip, narrow black wing borders and often a faint cell spot; female pale yellow to near white with lighter black markings

Below: seasonally variable; hindwings yellow to near white with pinkish red spot on outer margin (often absent on male) and several small, subtle spots or patches; winter-form darker yellow with additional pattern elements and pink wing fringe

Sexes: similar, although female is paler

Egg: white, laid singly on host leaves

Larva: green with thin, lateral cream-white stripe

Larval Host Plants: primarily Partridge Pea

Habitat: open, disturbed sites including roadsides, pastures, utility easements, vacant fields, agricultural land and sparse woodland trails

Broods: one or more generations

Abundance: uncommon to locally common

Compare: Dainty Sulphur (pg. 321) is generally smaller with a prominent black bar along the trailing margin of the dorsal forewing, olive-green scaling on the yellow dorsal hindwing and a distinct black postmedian spot on the ventral forewing.

Visitor

Jan. Feb. Mar. Apr. May June July Aug. Sept. Oct. Nov. Dec.

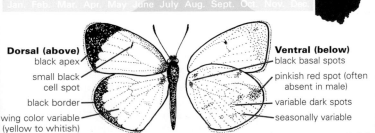

Dorsal (above)
black apex
small black cell spot
black border
wing color variable (yellow to whitish)

Ventral (below)
black basal spots
pinkish red spot (often absent in male)
variable dark spots
seasonally variable

Male   Winter   Larva

Comments: The only Ohio sulphur with pointed
forewings, the Dogface is named after the unique pattern on the dorsal surface of each forewing that
resembles (with some imagination) the head of a dog
in profile. Its distinctive pattern is visible only during
flight; adults rest and feed with wings tightly closed.
Adults have a strong, rapid flight but frequently stop to
nectar. It is an uncommon vagrant or temporary seasonal colonist to Ohio. Its presence is highly sporadic
and varies considerably from year to year. While the
majority of sightings are of isolated individuals, small
and highly localized colonies may be encountered.

Southern Dogface
Zerene cesonia

Family/Subfamily: Whites and Sulphurs (Pieridae)/ Sulphurs (Coliadinae)

Wingspan: 1.9–2.5" (4.8–6.4 cm)

Above: yellow; forewing pointed with broad, black margin highly scalloped to form image of dog's head in profile, single back cell spot and increased black scaling on basal area; hindwing has narrow black margin

Below: hindwings seasonally variable; summer-form is yellow with two small silver spots; winter-form has increased rosy pink scaling

Sexes: similar, although black markings duller and less extensive on female

Egg: white, laid singly on host leaves

Larva: variable; plain green to green with orange lateral stripe and transverse black and yellow stripes

Larval Host Plants: False Indigo, White Prairie Clover, Alfalfa and clovers

Habitat: open, sunny sites including pastures, meadows, alfalfa or clover fields, roadsides and overgrown fields

Broods: one or more generations

Abundance: rare; localized

Compare: All other sulphurs in Ohio lack the pointed forewing apex.

Stray

Jan. Feb. Mar. Apr. May June July Aug. Sept. Oct. Nov. Dec.

male

Dorsal (above)
pointed apex
black cell spot
dog's head shaped in yellow surrounded by black

Ventral (below)
seasonally variable; yellow to heavily dusted with pink scales

325

Male

White-form female
pg. 317

Larva

Comments: Like its close relative the Orange Sulphur with which it is often flies, this aggressive colonizer has likely benefitted from the spread of agriculture and human land use practices. Although it may be encountered in just about any open habitat, it is generally most abundant in commercial clover or alfalfa fields where it may occasionally become a pest. It is sexually dimorphic and seasonally variable. Both yellow and white-form females are common and adults produced under cool, early spring or late fall conditions tend to be smaller and darker below than those of the summer generations. Adults have a quick, erratic flight.

Clouded Sulphur
Colias philodice

Family/Subfamily: Whites and Sulphurs (Pieridae)/ Sulphurs (Coliadinae)

Wingspan: 1.90–2.75" (4.8–7.0 cm)

Above: clear lemon yellow with bold, solid black wing borders and a prominent black forewing cell spot; hindwing has a central orange spot

Below: yellow to greenish yellow; row (often faint or occasionally absent) of dark submarginal spots; pink wing fringes; hindwing has central red-rimmed silvery spot and adjacent smaller satellite spot

Sexes: dissimilar; female is less vibrant, often has more black scaling and broader black borders enclosing yellow spots; also has a common white form

Egg: white, laid singly on host leaves

Larva: blue-green with a lateral cream stripe marked in black below and often containing faint red dashes

Larval Host Plants: Alfalfa, Red Clover, White Clover and White Sweet Clover

Habitat: open, sunny sites including roadsides, meadows, alfalfa fields, parks, pastures and home gardens

Broods: multiple generations

Abundance: rare to occasional

Compare: Orange Sulphur (pg. 277) has at least some orange scaling above.

Resident

Jan. Feb. Mar. Apr. May June July Aug. Sept. Oct. Nov. Dec.

male

Dorsal (above)
black spot
yellow with no orange scaling
smooth black border
orange spot

Ventral (below)
two silvery spots
pink fringe
black dusting on hindwing
partial postmedian row of dark spots

Male

Female **Female** **Larva**

Comments: The large Cloudless Sulphur has a fast, powerful flight. An abundant resident of the Deep South, it regularly disperses northward to temporarily colonize much of the eastern U.S. each year, but is an uncommon and sporadic visitor to Ohio. Its presence often depends on past favorable winter weather. As fall approaches, large numbers of individuals undergo a massive southward migration to the Florida peninsula. The annual event is one of the Southeast's most impressive natural phenomena. Adults have an extremely long proboscis and can feed at many long, tubular flowers inaccessible to other butterflies.

Cloudless Sulphur
Phoebis sennae

Family/Subfamily: Whites and Sulphurs (Pieridae)/ Sulphurs (Coliadinae)

Wingspan: 2.2–2.8" (5.6–7.1 cm)

Above: unmarked bright lemon yellow; female has broken black wing borders and black forewing spot

Below: male is greenish yellow with virtually no markings; female is yellow with pinkish brown markings and several small silver spots in center of each wing; seasonally variable; winter-form adults more heavily marked

Sexes: similar, although female is more heavily marked

Egg: white, laid singly on host leaves or flower buds

Larva: green or yellow with broad lateral yellow stripe marked with blue spots or transverse bands

Larval Host Plants: various wild and ornamental cassia species including Partridge Pea, Wild Senna and Maryland Senna

Habitat: open, disturbed sites including roadsides, vacant fields, agricultural land, parks and gardens

Broods: two or more generations

Abundance: rare to uncommon

Compare: Clouded Sulphur (pg. 327) and Orange Sulphur (pg. 277) are smaller, have a solid black cell spot on the forewing and broad, solid black wing margins.

Stray

Jan. Feb. Mar. Apr. May June July Aug. Sept. Oct. Nov. Dec.

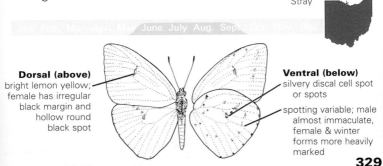

Dorsal (above)
bright lemon yellow; female has irregular black margin and hollow round black spot

Ventral (below)
silvery discal cell spot or spots

spotting variable; male almost immaculate, female & winter forms more heavily marked

329

Male

Female

Dark-form female pg. 67

Female

Dark-form female

Larva

Comments: Easily recognized by its bold, black stripes and bright yellow wings, the Eastern Tiger Swallowtail is spectacular in pattern and size. Adults have a strong, agile flight and often soar high in the treetops. Although fond of woodlands and waterways, it is equally at home in more urban areas and is a conspicuous garden visitor. Unlike many other swallowtails, the adults seldom flutter their wings while feeding. They instead rest on the blossom with their colorful wings outstretched. Dark-form females mimic the toxic Pipevine Swallowtail to gain protection from predators. Males often congregate at moist earth or animal dung.

Eastern Tiger Swallowtail
Papilio glaucus

Family/Subfamily: Swallowtails (Papilionidae)/ Swallowtails (Papilioninae)

Wingspan: 3.5–5.5" (8.9–14.0 cm)

Above: yellow with black forewing stripes and broad black wing margins; single row of yellow spots along outer edge of each wing

Below: yellow with black stripes and black wing margins; hindwing margins have increased blue scaling and a single submarginal row of yellow-orange, crescent-shaped spots; abdomen yellow with black stripes

Sexes: dissimilar; male always yellow but females have two color forms; yellow female has increased blue scaling in black hindwing border; dark-form female is mostly black with extensive blue hindwing markings

Egg: green, laid singly on upper surface of host leaves

Larva: green; enlarged thorax and two small false eyespots

Larval Host Plants: Wild Cherry, Black Cherry, ash and Tulip Tree

Habitat: deciduous forests, woodland margins, suburban gardens, urban parks, old fields, pastures, roadsides, alfalfa fields

Broods: multiple generations

Abundance: occasional to common

Compare: Yellow-form unique.

Resident

Jan. Feb. Mar. Apr. May June July Aug. Sep. Oct. Nov. Dec.

male

Dorsal (above)
yellow with black stripes

wide black border

yellow spots

long tail

Ventral (below)
yellow-orange spots

blue scaling

331

VERY RARE STRAYS

The following list of nine butterflies includes those that are considered to be very rare strays to Ohio from other areas. They are known only from isolated or very infrequent records. Nonetheless, they have the potential to be found within the state. It is likely that several other species will be added to this list in years to come, especially with the growing interest in butterfly watching and the Ohio Lepidopterists' Monitoring Network.

Marine Blue . . . . *Leptotes marina*

Gulf Fritillary . . . . *Agraulis vanillae*

Great Purple Hairstreak . . . . *Atlides halesus*

Queen . . . . *Danaus gilippus*

Bell's Roadside-Skipper . . . . *Amblyscirtes belli*

Brazilian Skipper . . . . *Calpodes ethlius*

Eufala Skipper . . . . *Lerodea eufala*

Long-tailed Skipper . . . . *Urbanus proteus*

Southern Skipperling . . . . *Copaeodes minima*

BUTTERFLY SOCIETIES

Butterfly societies are a great way to learn more about butterflies and moths in Ohio. They also provide resources to make valuable contacts, share your enthusiasm and get out into the field.

The Lepidopterists' Society
http://alpha.furman.edu/~snyder/snyder/lep/

North American Butterfly Association (NABA) www.naba.org

Ohio Lepidopterists www.ohiolepidopterists.org

PLANTS FOR YOUR BUTTERFLY GARDEN

The following are some recommended adult nectar sources and larval hosts for an Ohio butterfly garden. Most of the species are readily available at most retail garden centers or native plant nurseries. Before purchasing any landscape plant, always inquire with your local nursery personnel as to the specific soil, light, and care requirements needed for optimal growth and maintenance. Additionally, it is also a good idea to understand the plant's growth habit and eventual size at maturity before placing it in the ground. Visit a demonstration garden, a neighbor's yard or a nearby botanical garden to see how the plant looks after it has had a chance to grow a bit. Finally, remember that pesticides are not recommended for any butterfly garden as they can harm the very organisms you wish to attract. Consider using beneficial insects or insecticidal soap first before resorting to more extreme measures. If pesticides are required, always treat pest problems on a local level by applying treatment only to the infested plant and being careful of drift to neighboring vegetation.

Adult Nectar Sources
Herbaceous Perennials
Yarrow *(Achillea millefolium)*

Fragrant Giant Hyssop *(Agastache foeniculum)*

Indian Hemp *(Apocynum cannabinum)*

Swamp Milkweed *(Asclepias incarnata)*

White Swamp Milkweed *(Asclepias perennis)*

Showy Milkweed *(Asclepias speciosa)*

Common Milkweed *(Asclepias syriaca)*

Butterfly Weed *(Asclepias tuberosa)*

New England Aster *(Aster novae-angliae)*

False Aster *(Boltonia asteroides)*

334

Tickseed Coreopsis (Coreopsis lanceolata)
Tall Coreopsis (Coreopsis tripteris)
Purple Prairie Clover (Dalea purpurea)
Pale Purple Coneflower (Echinacea pallida)
Purple coneflower (Echinacea purpurea)
Rattlesnake Master (Eryngium yuccifolium)
Spotted Joe-Pye Weed (Eupatorium maculateum)
Common Boneset (Eupatorium perfoliatum)
Joe-Pye Weed (Eupatorium purpureum)
Blanket Flower (Gaillardia pulchella)
Western Sunflower (Helianthus occidentalis)
Rough Blazing Star (Liatris aspera)
Dotted Blazing Star (Liatris punctata)
Gayfeather (Liatris pycnostachya)

Marsh Blazing Star (Liatris spicata)
Cardinal Flower (Lobelia cardinalis)
Wild Bergamot (Monarda fistulosa)
Horsemint (Monarda punctata)
Summer Phlox (Phlox paniculata)
Gray-headed Coneflower (Ratibida pinnata)
Black-eyed Susan (Rudbeckia hirta)
Brown-eyed Susan (Rudbeckia triloba)
Cup Plant (Silphium perfoliatum)
Prairie Dock (Silphium terebinthinacium)
Stiff Goldenrod (Solidago rigida)
Showy Goldenrod (Solidago speciosa)
Blue Vervain (Verbena hastata)
Common Ironweed (Vernonia fasciculata)
New York Ironweed (Vernonia noveboracensis)
Culver's Root (Veronicastrum virginicum)

Shrubs and Trees
Bottlebrush Buckeye (Aesculus parviflora)
Red Buckeye (Aesculus pavia)
False Indigo (Amorpha fruticosa)
Butterfly Bush (Buddleia davidii)
Bluebeard (Caryopteris x chandonenis)
New Jersey Tea (Ceonothus americanus)
Buttonbush (Cephalanthus occidentalis)
Redbud (Cercis canadensis)

Sweet Pepperbush (Clethra alnifolia)
Dogwood (Cornus spp.)
Virginia Willow (Itea virginica)
Ninebark (Physocarpus opulifolius)
Black Cherry (Prunus serotina)
Chokecherry (Prunus virginiana)
Wild Azalea (Rhododendron canescens)
Viburnum (Viburnum spp.)
Chaste Tree (Vitex agnus-castus)

Annuals
Ageratum (Ageratum houstonianum)
Spider Plant (Cleome hasslerana)
Dianthus (Dianthus chinensis)
Globe Amaranth (Gomphrena globosa)
impatiens (Impatiens spp.)
Sweet Alyssum (Lobularia maritima)

Flowering Tobacco (Nicotiana alata)
Pentas (Pentas lanceolata)
Drummond Phlox (Phlox drummondii)
Tropical Sage (Salvia coccinea)
Mexican sunflower (Tithonia spp.)
Verbena (Verbena X hybrida)
Zinnia (Zinnia elegans)

Larval Host Plants

acacia (Acacia spp.)

Alfalfa (Medicago sativa)

Amaranth, Spiny (Amaranthus spinosus)

angelica (Angelica spp.)

Arrowwood, Southern (Viburnum dentatum)

Ash, Prickly (Zanthoxylum americanum)

Ash, Wafer (Ptelea trifoliata)

ashes (Fraxinus spp.)

Aspen, Quaking (Populus tremuloides)

aspens (Populus spp.)

Aster, Bushy (Aster dumosus)

Aster, Flat-topped White (Aster umbellatus)

Aster, Frost (Aster pilosus)

Aster, Smooth Blue (Aster laevis)

asters (Aster spp.)

Azalea, Flame (Rhododendron calendulaceum)

Basswood, American (Tilia americana)

bean family (Fabacea)

Beech, American (Fagus gandiflora)

beggarweeds (Desmodium spp.)

bentgrass (Agrostis spp.)

birches (Betula spp.)

bittercress (Cardamine spp.)

Bitternut (Juglans cinerea)

blueberries (Vaccinium spp.)

Blueberry, Blue Ridge (Vaccinium vacillans)

Blueberry, Highbush (Vaccinium corymbosum)

bluegrass (Poa spp.)

Bluegrass, Kentucky (Poa pratensis)

Bluestem, Big (Andropogon gerardii)

Bluestem, Little (Schizachyrium scoparium)

bluestems (Andropogon spp.)

Bride's Feathers (Aruncus dioicus)

Canarygrass, Reed (Phalaris arundinacea)

Carpetgrass, Broadleaf (Axonopus compressus)

Carpetweed, Green (Mollugo verticillata)

carrot family (Apiaceae) includes dill, fennel and parsley

Cassia species (Cassia spp.)

Cherry, Black (Prunus serotina)

Cherry, Wild (Prunus virginiana)

Chestnut, American (Castanea dentata)

Cinquefoil, Canada (Potentilla canadensis)

citrus (Citrus spp.)

Clover, Red (Trifolium pratense)

Clover, White (Trifolium repens)

Clover, White Prairie (Dalea candida)

Clover, White Sweet (Melilotus alba)

clovers (Trifolium spp.)

clovers, bush (Lespedeza spp.)

clovers, prairie (Dalea spp.)

clovers, sweet (Melilotus spp.)

Cohosh, Black (Cimicifuga racemosa)

Columbine, Wild (Aquilegia canadensis)

composites (Asteraceae)

Coneflower, Cut-leaf (Rudbecia lanciniata)

cordgrass (Spartina spp.)

Cottonwood (Populus deltoides)

Crabgrass, Slender (Digitaria filiformis)

crabgrasses (Digitaria spp.)

Croton, Silver (Croton argyranthemus)

Crownbeard, White (Verbesina virginica)

cudweeds (Gnaphalium spp.)

Cutgrass, Giant (Zizaniopsis milacea)

Cutgrass, Rice (Leersia oryzoides)

Cutgrass, Southern (Leersia hexandra)

Deertongue (Dichanthelium clandestinum)

Dock, Curly (Rumex crispus)

Dock, Water *(Rumex verticillatus)*
Dogwood, Flowering *(Cornus florida)*
Dogwood, Gray *(Cornus racemosa)*
dogwoods *(Cornus spp.)*
Dutchman's Pipe *(Aristolochia macrophylla)*
Elm, American *(Ulmus americana)*
Elm, Winged *(Ulmus alata)*
elms *(Ulmus spp.)*
Fescue, Red *(Festuca rubra)*
foxglove, false *(Agalinus spp.)*
Fresce, Tall *(Lolium arundinaceum)*
goatsbeard *(Aruncus dioicus)*
Goatweed *(Croton argyranthemus)*
gooseberries *(Ribes spp.)*
Grass, Bermuda *(Cynodon dactylon)*
Grass, Indian *(Sorghastrum nutans)*
Grass, Purpletop *(Tridens flavus)*
Grass, St. Augustine *(Stenotaphrum secundatum)*
Grass, Timothy *(Phleum pratense)*
grasses *(Poaceae)*
Gravelweed *(Verbesina helianthoides)*
Hackberry, Common *(Celtis occidentalis)*
Hackberry, Dwarf *(Celtis tenuifolia)*
hackberries *(Celtis spp.)*
hawthorn *(Crataegus spp.)*
Hazelnut, Beaked *(Corylus cornuta)*
heath family *(Ericaceae)*
Hickory, Bitternut *(Carya cordiformis)*
Hickory, Pignut *(Carya glabra)*
Hickory, Shagbark *(Carya ovata)*
hickories *(Carya spp.)*
hollies *(Ilex spp.)*
Hollyhock *(Althaea rosea)*
Hop, Common *(Humulus lupulus)*
Huckleberry, Black *(Gaylussacia baccata)*
Indigo, Blue Wild *(Baptisia australis)*
Indigo, False *(Amorpha fruticosa)*
Indigo, White Wild *(Baptisia alba)*
Indigo, Wild *(Baptisia tinctoria)*

knotweed *(Polygonum spp.)*
Lamb's Quarters *(Chenopidium album)*
Laurel, Mountain *(Kalmia latifolia)*
Leatherleaf *(Chamaedaphne calyculata)*
legumes *(Fabaceae)*
Locust, Black *(Robinia pseudoacacia)*
Locust, Honey *(Gleditsia triacanthos)*
Lousewort, Canadian *(Pedicularis canadensis)*
lovegrass *(Eragrostis spp.)*
Lupine, Wild *(Lupinus perennis)*
lupin *(Lupinus spp.)*
mallow family *(Malvaceae spp.)*
Mallow, Common *(Malva neglecta)*
mannagrass *(Glyceria spp.)*
Mannagrass, Fowl *(Glyceria striata)*
mesquite *(Prosopis spp.)*
milk peas *(Galactia spp.)*
milkweed family *(Asclepias spp.)*
Milkweed, Common *(Asclepias syriaca)*
Milkweed, Swamp *(Asclepias incarnata)*
Milkvetch, Canadian *(Astragalus canadensis)*
milkvetch *(Astragalus spp.)*
mustard family *(Brassicaceae)*
Mustard, Garlic *(Alliaria officinalis)*
Mustard, Wild *(Brassica campestris)*
Nettle, Canadian Wood *(Laportea canadensis)*
Nettle, False *(Boehmeria cylindrica)*
Nettle, Stinging *(Urtica dioica)*
nettles *(Urtica spp.)*
Oak, Black *(Quercus velutina)*
Oak, Blackjack *(Quercus marilandica)*
Oak, Northern Red *(Quercus rubra)*
Oak, Post *(Quercus stellata)*
Oak, Red *(Quercus rubra)*
Oak, Scrub *(Quercus ilicifolia)*
Oak, White *(Quercus alba)*
oaks *(Quercus spp.)*

Oatgrass, Poverty (Danthonia spicata)
Orchardgrass (Dactylis glomerata)
panic grasses (Panicum spp.)
Parsnip, Wild (Pastinaca sativa)
passion flowers (Passiflora spp.)
pawpaws (Asimina spp.)
Pea, Partridge (Cassia fasciculata)
Peanut, Hog (Amphicarpa bracteata)
Pellitory (Parietaria floridana)
Peppergrass, Field (Lepidium campestre)
Peppergrass, Virginia (Lepidium virginicum)
Pepperweed, Common (Lepidium densiflorum)
Pine, Eastern White (Pinus strobus)
Pine, Loblolly (Pinus taeda)
Pine, Pitch (Pinus rigida)
Pine, Shortleaf (Pinus echinata)
Pine, Virginia (Pinus virginiana)
pines (Pinus spp.)
Pipevine, Wooly (Aristolochia tomentosa)
pipevines (Aristolochia spp.)
Plantain, Narrowleaf (Plantago lanceolata)
plantains (Plantago spp.)
Plum, American (Prunus americana)
Plumegrass, Silver (Erianthus alopecuroidum)
poplars (Populus spp.)
pussy-toes (Antennaria spp.)
Queen Anne's Lace (Daucus carota)
Radish, Wild (Raphanus raphanistrum)
Ragwort, Round-leaf (Senecio obovatus)
Redcedar, Eastern (Juniperus virginiana)
Reed, Common (Phragmites australis)
Rice, Annual Wild (Zizania aquatica)
rockcress (Arabis spp.)
rose family (Rosacea)
Sassafras (Sassafras albidum)
scarlet-pea (Indigofera spp.)

sedge family (Cyperaceae)
Sedge, Beaked (Carex rostrata)
Sedge, Hairy (Carex lacustris)
Sedge, Shoreline (Carex hyalinolepis)
Sedge, Upright (Carex stricta)
sedges (Carex spp.)
Senna, Maryland (Cassia marilandica)
Senna, Wild (Cassia hebecarpa)
serviceberry (Amelanchier spp.)
Shepherd's Purse (Capsella bursa-pastoris)
Shorthusk, Bearded (Brachyelytrum erectum)
Sida (Sida acuta)
Snakeroot, Virginia (Aristolochia serpentaria)
Sneezeweed (Helenium autumnale)
Sorrel, Sheep (Rumex acetosella)
Spanish Needles (Bidens alba)
Sparkleberry (Vaccinium arboreum)
Spicebush (Lindera benzoin)
Sugarberry (Celtis laevigata)
Sumac, Staghorn (Rhus typhina)
Sumac, Winged (Rhus copallina)
sumacs (Rhus spp.)
sunflowers (Helianthus spp.)
Sweet Everlasting (Gnaphalium obtusifolium)
Switchgrass (Panicum virgatum)
Tea, Mexican (Chenopidium ambrosiodes)
Tea, New Jersey (Ceanothus americana)
Thistle, Swamp (Cirsium muticum)
thistles (Cirsium spp.)
toadflax (Linaria spp.)
Toothwort, Cut-leaf (Dentaria laciniata)
toothworts (Dentaria spp.)
Tulip Tree (Liriodendron tulipifera)
Turtlehead (Chelone glabra)
vegetables (broccoli, cabbage, cauliflower, turnips and others)
Velvetgrass, Common (Holcus lanatus)

Vetch, Carolina *(Vicia caroliniana)*
Vetch, Crown *(Coronilla varia)*
vetch, milk *(Astragalus spp.)*
vetches *(Vinca spp.)*
viburnum *(Viburnum spp.)*
Violet, Bird's-foot *(Viola pedata)*
violets *(Viola spp.)*
Walnut, Black *(Juglans nigra)*
walnuts *(Juglans spp.)*
Whitegrass *(Leersia virginica)*
Willow, Black *(Salix nigra)*
Willow, Carolina *(Salix caroliniana)*
Willow, Weeping *(Salix babylonica)*
willows *(Salix spp.)*
Wing-stem *(Verbesina alternifolia)*
wisterias *(Wisteria spp.)*
Woodoats, Indian *(Chasmanthium latifolium)*
Woolgrass *(Scirpus cyperinus)*
Yellowrocket, Garden *(Barbarea vulgaris)*

CHECKLIST/INDEX

Use the boxes to check the butterflies you've seen.

ABOUT THE AUTHOR

Jaret C. Daniels, Ph.D., is a professional nature photographer and entomologist at the University of Florida specializing in the ecology and conservation biology of Lepidoptera. He has authored numerous scientific papers, popular articles and books on butterflies, insects, wildlife conservation and butterfly gardening. He currently lives in Gainesville, Florida, with his wife Stephanie.